THROUGH THE EYES OF THE
ANGELS

Your fight is not against flesh and blood, but against the principalities, and powers, against the powers of this dark world and spiritual forces of evil in the heavenly realms.

(Ephesians 6:12)

WARNING

This book will challenge you and your beliefs. It gives you a unique perspective on the Word of God written in the New Testament.

Some readers may find some of the content written in this book to be controversial and possibly offensive. It was not the author's intention in anyway to offend any person's belief or faith. This book is the author's own interpretation of events written in the gospels.

Illustration of angels: Justin Martin Front cover by: Mystic Art Design

Copyright © 2019 John Matthews

*Published by Ematt Publishing
website.emattpublishing.com*

GW00544705

JON MATTHEWS

ABOUT THE AUTHOR

Jon Matthews, raised and lives in the East End of London, married with three children. He is a highly respected and sought-after teacher. Through his unique approach and insights of the Word of God, thousands of people have committed their lives to Christ because of his Bible studies. He has a unique gift of showing and explaining the Word in a very plain and simple way, that the hearer can see Jesus as He really is. He is well known for saying... "Too many people are rejecting Christ because all we do is to preach at them. We must understand that the average person on the street does not care how many Scriptures you know. Jesus is now re-presenting Himself to the world, to this new generation. All we need to do is to show them how relevant the Bible is to today's society."

THROUGH THE EYES OF THE
ANGELS

I want to say a big thank you to the following people:

First, to my wife, Angela
You are the best thing that ever happened to me. I'm very blessed that you're my wife, to be with someone as beautiful, intelligent, kind, and loving as you. I love you and I thank you for all the wonderful things you do for me and the kids, our three boys Eliott, Ethan and Eddison, so proud to be your dad, and to mum Delrose Marrett I love you all very much.

Also, I'd like to say a special thank you to
Bishop Wayne Malcolm & Maryla Abraham for the inspiration to write the Christmas nativity play from the perspective of the angels. When I first wrote it as a play, it was called **"Seen of Angels"**

Thank you to:
Cassandra Jones & family
Devron & Vanessa Cariba
Karen Allen
My niece Robbi Ikhinmwin & family

To Linton Beckels & Lipson Francis.
Two of my best friends, **'Seen of Angels'** would have never happened without you both, this is for you. May the Lord keep you both in His bosom until we meet again.

You're always in our hearts.
REST IN PEACE.

Above all, I'd like to thank my heavenly father Jesus Christ, without whom all this would not have been possible.

Illustration of angels: Justin Martin
Front cover by: Mystic Art Design

ematt publishing
126 Queenswood Gardens • London E11 3SG
emattpublishing.com • sales@emattpublishing.com
Tel: +44 20 7101 3397 • +44 775 345 8472

CONTENTS

THROUGH THE EYES OF THE ANGELS

Angels are heavenly creatures who carry out God's plans and desires. They have a variety of tasks because God has a variety of plans. It is the task of angels to do the will of God.

GABRIEL:
One of the Holy angels, who is over the garden, serpents and Cherubims. He prays and intercedes for mankind.

MICHAEL:
One of the Holy angels, namely the one put in charge of the best part of humankind, in charge of the nation.

RAGUEL:
One of the Holy angels, who executes judgement on the world and on fallen angels.

URIEL:
One of the Holy angels; namely the Holy angel that looks upon the spirits of men, that guides them in the path of righteousness.

SARAQAEL:
One of the Holy angels; is over spirits which sin and over the spirits of the children of men that transgress.

RAPHAEL:
One of the Holy Angels; the healer, who is over the spirits of men that is suffering and being afflicted.

REMIEL:
One of the Holy Angels, is over those who rise against the name of the Lord.

ZOTIEL:
One of the Holy Angels; the warrior that protects the holy things of God. The guardian of the tree of life back in the garden of Eden.

As a Christian, I find it extraordinary that most of us really don't understand when the Bible says that Jesus took our place and died for us. We don't really comprehend what that really means. Sometimes it is very difficult to have a true understanding of something that has a spiritual implication to it, but if you take the same scenario and bring it into the natural world, it begins to make perfect sense.

A TRUE STORY!

Two brothers grew up in the heart of Harlem, New York, they were very close siblings. The older always looked after this younger brother, because their mother died when they were very young.

The older brother did the best he could in raising his little brother. One day the younger brother got involved in a gang, and he killed someone.

Knowing that his older brother will be furious, he went home, took off the blood stain shirt packed his bags and left town. The older brother came home only to find a blood stain shirt on the floor. At the same time he hears the sound of police siren outside.

Knowing that his young brother has done something very wrong and not wanting him to go to prison, he quickly changed his shirt and put on his brother's shirt. The police came knocking at his door and found him with the blood stain shirt on. He was arrested found guilty and he got the death penalty.

Sometime past, with several attempts from the young brother to get in touched with his older brother, he returned to town but only to find out that his older brother had been punished for his crime. The guilt was too much to bare, so he went to the police station to give himself up, and told them that his brother did not commit the crime it was him.

To his amazement the policeman said, '**Son**, we know you committed that crime but the LAW say that we can't punish someone twice for the same crime. Your brother took your place

YOU ARE FREE TO GO...

THROUGH THE EYES OF THE ANGELS

And without controversy great
is the mystery of godliness:
God was manifest in the flesh,
justified in the Spirit,

SEEN OF ANGELS,

preached unto the Gentiles,
believed on in the world,
received up into glory.

(1 Timothy 3:16)

This is a story, a story of old of how

God left his angels and his heavenly throne.

He came as a baby to live with his own,

through the eyes of the angels

we shall all understand.

The Celestial City

This story began over two thousand years ago beyond the clouds in the heavens. There lies the Kingdom of God. Deep within the Kingdom resides The Celestial City. The city possesses the glory of God; its brilliance is like a precious jewel, like a stone of crystal-clear jasper. The walls were great and high and it had twelve gates and at each gate had twelve angels guarding it. There were three gates on the east, three on the north, three on the south and three on the west.

The city is laid out as a square; its length is as great as its breadth. It measured about one and half thousand miles square. The foundation of the city was decorated with all kinds of precious stones.

The first foundation was Jasper, the second, Sapphire; the third, Chalcedony; the fourth, Emerald; the fifth, Sardonyx; the sixth, Sardius; the seventh, Chrysolite; the eighth, Beryl; the ninth, Topaz; the tenth, Chrysoprase; the eleventh, Jacinth and the twelfth, Amethyst. The city walls were ordained with twelve gates; each individual gate was made of one pearl. The streets of the city were pure gold yet was transparent like glass. The city had no need of the sun or the moon to shine, for the glory of God illuminated it, always.

Suddenly, from the four corners of the Celestial City the voice of an angel echoed through it as he summoned the host of heaven together. "Hark ye herald angels; come hear the words of Archangel Gabriel, your captain." The angels began to gather together, pondering in anticipation awaiting news from their captain Gabriel.

The voice bellowing through the city came from Raguel, one of the holy angels, who executes judgement on the world and on fallen angels. A brave soldier, who has fought many battles; such bravery had earned him the position of lieutenant in the army of the Most High. Raguel had been ordered to assemble the host of heaven together. The order came from none other than, the Archangel himself.

There was uneasiness in the city, and no one was really sure what was happening, not even Raguel himself. "A lieutenant has no choice but to follow orders," he said, as he shouted again, "Hark ye herald angels; come hear the words of Archangel Gabriel, your captain." As he summoned the angels again his voice travelled through the city walls and streets. Again, he repeats! "Hark ye herald angels; come hear the words of Archangel Gabriel, your captain".

When all the angels gathered together in the centre of the city, Raguel stood tall looking into a sea of curious faces, whilst holding a firm grip on his own curiosity, then addresses them all. "We have been summoned here by the Archangel Gabriel who has an announcement of great importance. Behold our captain Gabriel, messenger and servant of the Most High God."

Suddenly the sound of trumpets saturated the whole city and as he made his entrance the angels bow their heads down low in respect. As brave as Raguel was, he bowed deeply as Gabriel's majestic figure towered over the rest of the angels. His gold breast-plated armour was shining brightly, reflecting the brightness of being in the presence of the Most High.

Gabriel wasn't just God's messenger; he was one of three archangels God had created in the beginning to serve Him. That was before the rebellion where the status of Archangel only belonged to Michael, Gabriel and their renegade brother, Lucifer. Gabriel was also the angel that the Lord put in charge of the Garden, the Serpents and the Cherubim's. And he prays and intercedes for mankind. He waited until all the angels were silent, not a sound could be heard. And then in his bold and stern voice Gabriel addresses the host of heaven.

Gabriel's Entrance

"Greetings heavenly host! Servants and guardians of the Most High God. I am Gabriel; I stand in the presence of God. I listen to His Holy words, the King of all creation sends me to every nation to bring the word of God. The Holy words of God." After his introduction he told the angels to stand at ease. He slowly began pacing up and down as if searching for the right words to say.

"Alas! I Gabriel have come, not with good tidings. For it is with great bewilderment and sorrow in my heart that I declare these words unto you." At the hearing of these words the angels began murmuring. But Gabriel continued, "I am afraid!" There was an unusual tension in his voice as if he was unable to find the right words to say. He cleared his throat, "I am afraid! I am afraid that our Lord God is about to leave us."

The angels are shocked at the news and a crescendo of murmuring filled every corner of the city. This sends everyone into a state of panic and fear. They began to voice their opinion on the news, which they had just heard. Someone shouted, "Leave? Leave? Where can the Master go? Heaven is His throne. He that has created the whole universe leaves us to go where?" And another angel said, "What? Are you sure?" Gabriel could see the frustration on their faces and tried to tone down his voice. "I believe," he said, "the Lord God wants to be with those humans." Someone shouted; "Those humans again! What is it about those humans that He would leave his throne and live among them?"

All of the angels wanting answers to their questions. "Gabriel, why?" asked another! "They're not like us, they're only mortals. How can this be?" The angels became very confused, unable to comprehend the thought of God leaving His heavenly throne. They all carried on talking, all at the same time. Someone said; "They hate Him; they don't even know that He exist, humans worship all kind of gods, they don't know the Creator. Archangel, He cannot leave us! No disrespect Archangel, what makes you so sure? How do you know this?" another angel asked.

The angels started murmuring amongst themselves and the noise grew louder and louder. Raguel clapped his hands and in a loud and sturdy voice...said! "Silence Before the archangel!" and immediately order returned. Gabriel looked around him seeing the sadness in the eyes of the angels and began to explain his discovery. "I Gabriel have been summoned on many occasions, before the throne of the Most High God. He has been sending me on missions to deliver messages to mankind.

"First; I delivered a message to a woman by the name of Elizabeth, who was married to a man by the name of Zechariah. They were childless because Elizabeth was not able to conceive, and they were both very old. I entered the temple to talk to Zechariah and when he saw me, he was very fearful but I said to him, 'Do not be afraid, Zechariah; your prayers has been heard. I am Gabriel. I stand in the presence of God and I have been sent to speak to you and to tell you this good news. Your wife Elizabeth will bear you a son; it is through him that the Lord God is preparing the way for His visitation to mankind. He would use the vessel of this mortal and you are to call him John. He will be a joy and delight to you, and many will rejoice because of his birth, for he will be great in the sight of the Lord. He is never to take wine or any other fermented drink and he will be filled with the Holy Spirit, even before he is born. He will bring back many of the people of Israel to the Lord their God. He will be in the spirit and power of Elijah, to make the people ready for the coming of the Lord.'

"And now! I have just returned from a mission, which has put the whole mystery into perspective. I think that the Lord God is about to leave us...."
Just then another angel came before Gabriel and said, "Archangel, are you quite sure about this, are you?"

Gabriel continues to explain his reasoning: "I was sent to a city called Nazareth, a town in Galilee, to a virgin pledged to be married to a man named Joseph, a descendant of David. The virgin's name was Mary. Mary was greatly troubled at my words and wondered what kind of greeting this might be. But the words my Master gave to me left questions for us all. I told her, 'Do not be afraid, Mary; you have found favour with God. You will conceive and give birth to a son, and you are to call him, Jesus. He will be great in the sight of man and will be called Emmanuel.'"

"Emmanuel?" Someone shouted! With a look of disbelief on their faces, the angels said one to another; Who is Emmanuel?

But Gabriel continued. "The Lord God will give Him the throne of His father David, and He will reign over Jacob's descendants forever; His Kingdom will never end." Mary asked, "How will this be, since I am a virgin?" "The Holy Spirit will come on you, and the power of the Most High will overshadow you. Therefore, the Holy One to be born will be called the Son of the Most High." At this point the host of heaven was shocked at the news. "The son of God!" they all uttered. "What son?"

Then suddenly the whole of heaven began to shake as if a volcano had erupted; the city darkened, the foundations of the heavens raged, the whole of heaven was moved violently, the lightning flashed, the thunder roared and all the fountains in the heavens were shaken up. All the angels gasped and stood in amazement. Gabriel stopped! A look of dismay came over his face as a sense of emptiness spread throughout the city. "It has happened!" he said, "The Lord God has gone."

The angels began to panic and looked at each other confused, not knowing what to say or do... They all stared at Gabriel looking for an explanation and understanding about what had just taken place. "You see," he said, "God shall be with man, He shall be one of them, He shall become a Son and He shall be called Emmanuel."

Suddenly the sound of trumpets once again filled the city and Remiel, one of the holy angels, who is over those who rise against the name of the Lord. In a loud voice announces the arrival of Michael the archangel. "Make way for the archangel Michael, captain and mighty warrior of the Most High God."

Michael, Lucifer and Gabriel, the three brothers that ruled the heavens, but at the fall of his brother Lucifer, God put Michael in charge of the best part of human-kind and in charge of the nations of the earth.
The angels calmed down and gathered together to hear what Michael had to say. Michael salutes Gabriel and tells the angels to stand at ease as he explains;

"Host of heaven, servants and protectors of His Majes-ty's throne. To Him that live forever and ever. I Michael, stand before you with strict instruction from the Most High. YES! It is true; our Lord God has gone. As cap-tain of the host, He has instructed me to summon you all together. We are to go down to earth to proclaim His glory and might, to two shepherds in the land of Israel in a small place called, Judaea and sing praises to His holy name." And with one voice all the angels said, "Blessed be His Holy Name."

Michael and the angels acknowledge each other with a bow as he takes his leave. The angels then gather around Gabriel, sad that their Lord had left them to be with mankind.

THROUGH THE EYES OF THE ANGELS

The Shepherds

Back on the earth, in the night hour, two shepherds are camping around a fire. Suddenly, the sound of angels singing from above cause them to look up in amazement, wondering where that sound was coming from. They became frightened, so the majestic Gabriel appeared before them. The two shepherds were shaking with fear. "Please sir! Do not hurt us," they said.

Gabriel approached them and said, "Do not be afraid, I am Gabriel, messenger of the Most High God. I bring good tidings of great joy to all mankind. For unto you this day in the city of David, a Saviour, which is Christ the Lord, is born. He shall be a sign unto you. You shall find the babe wrapped in swaddling clothes lying in a manger. Now go!" Gabriel points in the direction they must go to find the baby. Still trembling with fear, the shepherds said to one another, "Let's go to Bethlehem and see this thing, which the Lord has told us. Quickly let's go."

Soon the two shepherds arrived at the stable where Mary and Joseph were staying. As Mary and Joseph were making their way home, they had to stop, for Mary could no longer travel, she was pregnant and was about to give birth. They tried to find a place to have the baby, but none could be found. An innkeeper said to them, "All my rooms are full, I have none to give you, but if you'd like to, you can use my stable, it's warm and I'll get the wife to come and help you and bring you something to eat..." Joseph said thank you to the inn keeper, and there the baby was born in the stable and they laid him in a manger.

The baby was crying as angels softly sang to it. When the shepherds came into the stable they said, "We have come to pay homage to the Messiah, the new King of Israel. We have been told that He is the Saviour of the world. We were told by the angel to come here and we will see the child." Now! The Scripture has been fulfilled; "God has come to save us." The two shepherds walked towards the baby and fell down on their knees, worshipping him: As they stood back on their feet, one of the shepherds spoke to Mary and Joseph, "This is truly a miracle that this child, the son of God has come to earth. We must go and proclaim this to the world, Glory be to the Lord God, for indeed salvation has come to mankind." They kissed Mary's hand and said to her, "You are truly blessed, for indeed God has come to Israel." The two shepherds then bowed down and left the stable to proclaim the glory of the Lord.

When the shepherds left Mary and her husband she walked towards the manger, picked up her baby and began rocking him in her arms. The feeling of an over-whelming sense of fulfilment came over her, as she gazed into her son's eyes. She began shaking her head in amazement still some doubt in her mind whether all that has been declared about the child in her arms were true. She began questioning herself: "What kind of miracle is this? How can this be?" She looks at her baby as if asking him the questions, "Are you my God? Or are you my King? No! She hesitated; you are my baby.

"I have always been told that the Messiah would come; but I never thought you would use me." As she said that a smile came over her face. "Why did you choose someone like me? I'm but a simple girl, a maid that knew no man. But here I am today, a mother mild beholding God within my new born son. Oh! My soul magnifies you my Lord and my spirit rejoice in God my Saviour. You have picked me, the lowest of your maid-servants. You have done a great thing to me. The world will call me bless. Holy is your name." She looked again at her baby as her husband Joseph came over and put his arms around her, and the feeling of happiness filled her heart.

The Gathering

Deep down beneath the palace dungeon and beyond, a dark cringing little figure travels through the walls of the dungeon heading towards the gathering. "I mustn't be late," it says to itself. "The master will not be happy with the news I have to tell him." Zaqiel is a squirmy little demon barely three-foot-tall; he is the spirit and master of gossiping, always wants to know and be in everything. He has many friends and is highly respected in his circles. Making his way down towards the hollow chambers, where his master is waiting, he gasps for air as the smell of sulphur fills the atmosphere. "Must not show fear," he says, "the master feeds on fear and he can smell it a mile off. Stay calm," he said to himself, "everything will be okay."

As he entered into the hollow chamber, the hall was creeping with demons. "It seems like everyone is here. What's going on?" He asked someone.

"The MASTER has called this meeting, it seems that he has something important to say to us all. I see you're late, again, but you're lucky this time, the master hasn't started yet." said one of his close friends, Confucius. "How are you doing Deep?" he asked the demon Depression that was standing at the side of him. He then lifted up his hand to a friend. "Hi Lids great to see you again, talk later!" Lidsidious just gave Zaqiel that smiled as if to say, I'll see you much, much later. All his old friends are here tonight. He tries to squeeze in at the back, trying not to be noticed as he sneaked into the hall, just as his master Lucifer was turning around with a deep but loud groan that echoed through the chamber.

"It is time!" the voice got louder; "It is time, I said. It has been four hundred years and the God up there has been very quiet. Very quiet indeed! He hasn't said a word to any man, not since that prophet Malachi. No! Not one word, nothing! I thought that He had abandon mankind," said Lucifer. "This is my world, we control this land, but the prophecy foretold that He will return to this earth." He looked up to the heavens and said to his followers, "You all listen and listen well, I am the god of this world and no one dare move without my say so." He said, "Creatures of the night, keep your eyes open – let me know about anything that is unusual in the city."

As the master spoke, Zaqiel tries to push his way towards the front of the crowd. "Please let me pass, let me pass," with his squeaky little voice – "I have important news for the master," he shouted, unable to get through the crowd. "Master! Master!" he shouted. His master turned around trying to see where that sound was coming from, but unable to see anything apart from the rolls of bodies moving aside as Zaqiel tries to push his way through the crowded room.

"Move aside!" Shouted Lucifer, and all the demons moved as a dividing line was created and, as if out of nowhere, the master saw this little imp trying to get to the front.

"Master! Master!" said Zaqiel, "I have something to say."

"Speak up!" his master shouted. "This better be good, for your sake for interrupting me..."

"Yes master! There was something very unusual that happened last night." Zaqiel tried to talk but standing before the presence of Lucifer, his throat suddenly felt very dry. He continued, "One of our foot soldiers saw Gabriel and the host of heaven in Judaea."

"What!" Bellowed the master, "The host of heaven here? It has begun!" he said as if he was talking to himself. "Gabriel thinks he is clever, quietly coming into my world. We will see brother," he said; as anger came over his face.

"Listen to me you all," he shouted, "the host of heaven is here! The prophecy of that child has begun – that is the only reason why my so called brother Gabriel would be here." He then shouted like a mad man with a voice that rumbled through the whole chamber. "Find me that child, wherever he is... Find him! If you have to turn the whole country upside down, do so! I say, find me that child!"
Fear spread throughout the chamber –

"We haven't seen him so angry before," said Lidsidious to the demon he was standing next to.
"Yeah! He's gone totally mad..."

The Kings

After Jesus was born in a stable in Bethlehem of Judea, Mary and Joseph took the baby and went to their home, where the child grew in stature. At the age of two, kings from the east with their entourage came to Jerusalem asking; "Where is the one who has been born king of the Jews? We saw his star when it rose and have come to worship him."

When one of Herod's soldiers saw the crowds gathering, he went to Herod and said, "Sir! There's a crowd of foreigners who have entered the town."

"Foreigners?" asked Herod. "Yes Sir; they are kings; they say they have come to see the King of the Jews."

"What King?" Herod asked. "I am the only king in Judea." The people of Judea seeing such a vast number of foreigners coming into their town were afraid; "We have no army," they said, "Are we under siege?"

Herod ordered the soldier to bring the leaders to him – "How can they say that there is another king? What King?" With anger growing inside him, Herod called together all the people; the leaders of Judea, the chief priests and teachers of the law and asked them where the Messiah was to be born. "In Bethlehem in Judea," they replied, for this is what the prophet has written: But you, Bethlehem, in the land of Judah, are by no means least among the rulers of Judah; for out of you will come a ruler who will shepherd my people, Israel.

Herod called the kings secretly and asked them the exact time the star had appeared. He sent them to Bethlehem and said, "Go and search carefully for the child. When you have found him, report back to me, so that I too may go and worship him." Seeing all the treasures, a smile came across Herod's face and the thought went through his mind. He sniggered to himself. "All these treasures from these kings will be mine – I will be so rich, I'll be richer than Caesar himself." After their meeting with Herod, they went on their way. As night falls the kings agreed that they should wait until the morning to start their search again.

In the morning when they arose, the star they had seen went ahead of them, so the kings together with their entourage numbering about eighty-five people, followed the star until it stopped over Mary's house. "Where is the child?"

When they saw the star stopped, they were overjoyed. While Joseph the carpenter was working in his workshop, he saw strangers coming into his neighbourhood. Everyone in the neighbourhood came out to see all the strangers.

"Who are these foreigners?" they said to one another! "They are heading towards Joseph's house; do you see that?"

"These wagons are full of treasures. Is Joseph a king?" "Why all these treasures? I have counted at least twelve wagons," said another. "Where have all these visitors come from?" they all asked. Someone said, "They are foreigners from another land."

On coming towards the house, the kings got off their wagons and together walked towards Joseph's house. "Is this the house where the new king of Israel lives?" they asked.

Mary and Joseph stood at the front door of their house. Joseph asked, "What can we do for you sirs?"

"Is this the house of the new King of Israel?" they said. "For it was written in the Holy Scriptures; Oh, Bethlehem, are you not the least among the princes of Judah: For out of you shall come a Governor that shall rule my people, Israel. We have come to pay Him homage. Look! We have come with gifts and good tidings. We are seeking for the promised child, the one that they have said will change the destiny of the world. It has been written that the Messiah has been born and is now a young child. We have searched from the Far East to this place here. The star has guided us to this town of Bethlehem, to this house. Is the child here?"

The crowd outside, listening to all the kings' conversations, started murmuring – "No way, this is impossible – A King, here? In this god forsaken land?"

Someone said, "You must be joking." At this point Joseph invited the kings to come into the house where the young child Jesus was. When Mary showed them the young Jesus, they bowed down and worshiped him.

One king said, "Behold, my eyes have seen the salvation of the Lord. He has sent a light to lighten the path of his people. Hail, King of glory! He has robed himself in flesh; He has left his throne to dwell among us."

They continued to praise the child. "For unto us a child is born, unto us a son is given, and the government shall be upon his shoulder and his name shall be called, Wonderful, Counsellor, The mighty God, the everlasting Father and the Prince of Peace." And simultaneously they said, "Lord receives these humble gifts." Then they opened some of their treasures and presented him with gifts of gold, frankincense and myrrh. Another king said: "For you are truly the King of kings, Lord of lords, your glory fill all heaven and earth, for you have chosen the foolish thing of this world to confound the wise, and the weak things to confound the strong. Blessed be your holy name." After giving their salutations, the kings unloaded their gifts to the child, kissed Mary's hand and headed back to their countries.

That night while Raguel and Raphael was guarding the house, an angel from heaven came down with news from their captain Gabriel. Uriel, one of the Holy Angels, namely the holy angel that looks upon the spirits of men, that guides them in the path of righteousness. He was sent to earth to take an important message to Raguel. "Lieutenant Raguel, I have some urgent news for you from our captain Gabriel. He said

I am to inform you that the enemy is planning to kill the child. He said that you must tell the kings that they must not under any circumstances, go back to King Herod and disclosed the whereabouts of the child." When Uriel had delivered the message, Raguel said, "Uriel, you stay here with Raphael and guard the child, I will go and deliver this message to them."

When Raguel arrived at the camp, everyone was asleep. "Good!" he said. He entered the tent of the kings and began talking to them in the spirit while they slept. "Herod wants to kill the child; you must go back to your countries a different way, you and your people must travel to the north. By the time Herod wakes up you will be far-gone!"

Raguel got back to the house – "Raphael, Uriel it is done, now we must get the parents and child to safety." Raphael said, "I will talk to Joseph."
"We must leave now." Joseph rose from his sleep and then woke up Mary and said to her, "In my dream the Lord just told me that we must take Jesus and leave this place now, Herod is coming to kill him, and we must stay there until he tells us to come back. We must move quickly!" So they left the house in haste

and headed towards Egypt unknowing to them with the three angels by their side.

When the kings got up that morning, they said to one another, "Last night I had a dream that the Lord said we must not go back to Herod."

"That's strange," said the other kings, "We had the same dream."

THROUGH THE EYES OF THE

ANGELS

Kill All The Children

Baraqiel is a slimy worm of a demon. An evil spirit that loves inflicting pain on others, especially humans. "What is it now Baraqiel?" ask his master Lucifer.

"Well master, it's been two years and we have search high and low for this child but still no news from any of our foot soldiers."

"The child couldn't have just vanished," said Lucifer! "He must be found..."

"I think I have found him," said Baraqiel.

"Yesss!" Groan his master.

"You see, there are definitely some unusual activities going on in the town today." said Baraqiel as his master turned around to give him his full attention. "There are wagons and a large crowd of people, visitors from another land heading to Galilee claiming that they are looking for a King! And they are following a star." "Who are these people and where have they come from?"

"I do not know, apparently, their leaders are supposed to be kings. They have seen Herod and have gone to find the child."

"At last," said Lucifer, "we have got him. Now follow these people and bring me that child." Baraqiel, called for some more of their soldiers. "Now go and get that child, I want him dead!"

Baraqiel and his friends arrived at the house where the child was. He orders his demons to search high and low but they could not be found. "Where are they?" He shouted! "Find that child. They must be here!" All the demons searched the whole house but found nothing. "Oh no, my master is not going to be happy about this."

Baraqiel made his way back to the palace dungeon. Where his master awaits the news; "Well! What have you to report? Is he dead?"

"No master the child still lives –"

"Why?" Shouted Lucifer!

"Master, when we arrived the child had already gone."

"Noooo! This child MUST die!" He cried out in fury. "He will not get away from me this time. Baraqiel, summon Kokabiel, my most evil and treacherous demon, bring him here to me now."

"Yes master!" Within a moment Kokabiel arrived, bowing low as he came before his master.

"My good disciple, go, get into the mind of Herod, that bumbling fool and make him kill every male child in the land from two years and under. Spear not one, destroy them all!" said Lucifer. "He will not get away from me this time! Tonight! he shouted, as he slammed his fist on the table. This night! This child MUST DIE."

Kokabiel, travelled up into Herod's chamber and began attacking his mind. In the morning when Herod woke up and realised that he had been outwitted by the kings, he was furious! He gave orders to kill all the children in Bethlehem and its vicinity who were two years old and under. And so, the word of the prophet Jeremiah was fulfilled: A voice is heard in Ramah, weeping and great mourning, Rachel weeping for her children and refusing to be comforted, because her children were no more.

THROUGH THE EYES OF THE

The Missing Child

Several years has gone by since the birth of Jesus, and the sense of normality returned to Bethlehem. Lucifer and his demons are satisfied that several years ago they had killed the promised child. They reigned over all of Israel. His demonic forces possessed many hosts and all seemed well in the land.

Azazel is one of the evil spirits who has taught iniquity on the earth. He went to meet with his master about a situation that happened in the temple.

"Master!" he said, "Something unusual happen in the temple today!" "What?" said Lucifer, not really paying him much attention.

"I was sitting in the temple next to a group of priests and this young boy came in speaking as if he was one of the leaders, in fact, it seemed like he knew more than these leaders."

THROUGH THE EYES OF THE ANGELS

"What is all this about?" said Lucifer, "What boy? What is not normal?" He asked. Azazel continued; "This young boy could only be about twelve years old, where could he have gotten such knowledge? And when he spoke, it was with such authority. He was in the temple alone for about three days until his parents found him sitting in the midst of the doctors, both hearing and asking them questions. The temple was packed with people for the feast. I also saw two of the host of heaven in the temple standing near the boy."

"Were they with the boy?"

"I'm not quite sure sir! But there was something strange about that boy. It didn't feel right, just being near the boy, I felt something strange. What was even more strange was when the boy's mother asked him why he didn't stay with them. Why was he sitting there whilst they were out looking for him thinking that he was lost, why would he do that? The boy then said to his parents; 'Why are you looking for me? Do you not know that I must be about my father's business?'

"The boy parents and everyone that were near him were shocked and looked a bit confused when he spoke, so his parents grabbed him and took him home with them."

THROUGH THE EYES OF THE ANGELS **31**

"Maybe the boy just runaway from home," said his master! "Should I keep a close eye on this boy?"

"No," said Lucifer, "do not waste your time with him, a twelve-year-old boy can cause you no problem. As for the host of heaven, they must have been there for one of the leaders, so leave the boy alone, we have bigger fish to fry."

Twenty years has gone by and Lucifer summons his followers. Demons from the outermost part of Israel gathered together. "We have been ruling this world without interference from the God up there, and for the last four hundred years we have only had one little incident, that promise child who we killed. So, who is this now that is calling on his name?"

Tamiel said! "Master, we think this is a mad man."

"What do you mean, he is mad? Does one of our followers possess this man?"

"No master!"

"So why is he mad if we do not possess him?" said Lucifer. "Master! He is not normal. This man lives in the wilderness and he wears camel's hair for clothes with a leather belt around his waist. He only eats locusts and wild honey." "Are you quite sure we do not occupy this host?"

"Yes master! He seems to be speaking on behalf of the God up there. He is telling the people that they need to repent and be baptised. All the leaders hate him; he seems to be annoying them all."

"Who is he and where did he come from? In my world no one speaks of the God up there – No one!" Lucifer stopped for a moment as if he was in deep thought. "Is this man a Pharisee or Sadducee? Why is it only now that I'm hearing about this man?"

"I don't know master," said Tamiel, "but he doesn't act like any prophet we've seen before."

"Mmm! Keep a close eye on this man – if he starts giving us any trouble then destroy him. I will not have any so-called prophet wakening my people."

THROUGH THE EYES OF THE
ANGELS

The Wilderness

An evil spirit by the name Satael who has deceived mankind and love leading them into wickedness approached his master Lucifer.

"Master you know you told us to keep our eyes open for any unusual activities in Jerusalem? Well! Well! There is a-a-a!"

"Speak up you blubbering fool," said Lucifer.

"There is a man, not sure where he came from but one of our foot soldiers claimed that this mere mortal has changed water into wine."

"Wine?" shouted his master! "Wine you say? Impossible! Who is this mortal? Is he the one that lives in the wilderness wearing camel's hair for clothes?"

"No Master!"

"Then are you telling me that there is someone else in my world that we do not control? I need to know who this man is. Bring that soldier to me at once." Satael returned with this insignificant little demon. "Here he is master!"

"Well Soldier," said Lucifer, "what is this that I hear – that a man, a mere mortal has turned water into wine! Did you see this with your own eyes?"

"No master! We tried to get into the wedding where this man was, but we could not enter –"

"And why not?"

"Raguel and Raphael from the other side guarded the doors."

"Did you say Raguel and Raphael? Hmmm! Two of Michael's finest warriors. What are they doing here?"

"Master, Slimmer got in through the back door into the kitchen where his host was one of the servants and he heard everything, but that's not all master, this same man is now walking through the wilderness. Should we attack him?"

"No! I'll deal with this one myself – I wonder! Could it be?" Not finishing his sentence, he stood up to address his followers. "Now listen!" he shouted, "The host of heaven is here, be on the lookout as they are very cunning. Do not underestimate them, they might be few in numbers but are very wise. And as for this man who ever he is – I will deal with him myself..."

Lucifer came to the desert. "Well! Well! Well! Look who we have here - Raguel and Raphael, we meet again. Is my brother Michael still not fighting his own battles? Still sending infants to do a general's work I see! Are you still taking orders from that low-life? Who is it that you are supposed to be protecting this time, is he the one?"

Raphael, unable to control his emotions said, "If you are looking for a fight today Lucifer you have come to the right place."

With a voice as if to tease Raphael, Lucifer said, "Fight you? Oh no! I haven't come to fight with you, well! Not today! – Today, I've come for Him," as he points to Jesus.

"Leave him alone," said Raphael.

"NO! YOU know the rules – all men upon the earth belong to me, alive or dead. I know my rights."

"Who said?" replied Raphael!

"The law said and there's really nothing that you or anyone can do about it. Did you know by law you are trespassing on my property? This is my world you're standing in and there's not a man on earth who can stop me, so stand back and watch the master at work."

"Raphael, he is right, put back your sword," said Raguel!

"We can not touch him, we can only watch and pray that the Lord has the strength to see this through."

"But Raguel, the Lord is too weak to withstand an attack against Lucifer; he hasn't eaten for forty days."

"I am worried too Raphael," said Raguel, "but Lucifer is right, we have no power over him, this is his domain."

Lucifer approached Jesus and said, "If you are the Son of God, tell these stones to become bread."

Jesus answered, "It is written: 'Man shall not live on bread alone, but on every word that comes from the mouth of God.'"

Then he took Jesus to the holy city and had Him stand on the highest point of the temple. "If you are the Son of God," he said, "throw yourself down. For it is written: 'He will command his angels concerning you, and they will lift you up in their hands, so that you will not strike your foot against a stone.'"

But Jesus answered him saying, "It is also written: 'Do not put the Lord your God to the test.'"

Again, Lucifer took Him to a very high mountain and then showed Him all the kingdoms of the world and their splendour. "All these cities I will give to you," he said, "if you will bow down and worship me. It was given to me and I can give it to whomever I please."

Jesus said to him, "Get away from me, Satan! For it is written: 'Worship the Lord your God and serve him only.'"

Lucifer said to himself, who is this man? Who is this so-called prophet? He has rejected all my offers, he seems to be very strong, but he is human and all souls are mine. I will get back to him later. So, he left Jesus until another time.

"Raphael, quickly, Lucifer has gone," Raguel said, "I never thought that the Lord was going to make it. It was a tough call, but he didn't fall under the temptation of Lucifer, quickly, we need to attend to the Lord now."

The Celestial City

In the heavenly realm, within the Celestial City a number of years have now past and the angels are in discussion about how long the Lord God has been away
on the earth. There is growing concern about the Lord.
Saraqael, one of the holy angels, is over spirits who sin
in the spirit, and over the spirits of the children of men
that transgress, stands before Archangel Michael;

"What have you to report?" asks the archangel!

"Captain! It has been thirty years since the Lord's been
on the earth. We have watched over Him as his mortal
shell has grown into a man, but what I have just seen
is too much to bear. We sat here watching Him suffer
for forty days and forty nights without food, without
drink. We allowed the renegade Lucifer to be alone
with the Master in the wilderness; and we sat here
and did nothing. This is an abomination! We must do
something!"

The Archangel Michael stood up and said, "No! I have given you strict instructions; while the Lord is in His earthly vessel we cannot interfere."

"But captain, why?"

"Saraqael, I too do not fully understand the meaning of what is going on, but we must follow orders."

Just then, an angel comes running in with news from earth.

"Captain! Captain! I have just returned from the earth with news, some serious news. They have just killed the Lord's chosen one, the one they call John the Baptist."

"And the master?" asked Michael!

"The Lord has picked twelve followers, they are with Him night and day. But Archangel, there is tension growing among the people, and I have just seen legions of Lucifer's followers gathering in Jerusalem.... Sir, I am afraid for the Master".

The angels whisper among themselves, worried about what would become of their Master.

The angel Saraqael, feeling a sense of frustration, said, "There is a build-up of demonic forces gathering in Jerusalem, and we sit here and do nothing! Sir! We must do something."

Michael spoke to the angels with the sense of urgency. "We have Raguel, Raphael and Uriel on the ground, but I need you Saraqael, to assist Archangel Gabriel and keep close to the Master. Do not let him out of your sight and under no circumstances are you to engage in any warfare. Be alert! Be vigilant! But we must not interfere."

The City of Magdala

In the town of Magdala, a small fishing town on the western shore of the Sea of Galilee, there was a woman. She was a very beautiful woman; her eyes would pierce right through your very soul, one look from her and you were bewitched. She was a lady of the night; she understood the power of male desire and she made sure that they all found her irresistible.

Her appearance was that of a goddess and she had the ability of seduction. She seduced many in the village, man and women a like, and all wanted to be in her presence. She had great influence and manipulated many high officials and used her powers to control them all. Being such a wealthy woman, she had the whole town under her control. She led many people of Magdala in the similar way of Sodom and Gomorrah.

THROUGH THE EYES OF THE ANGELS

Meanwhile, deep down in their lair two demons were walking down toward the throne room. They had been summoned by none other than their master, Lucifer himself. As they entered into the room a voice said to them, "Have you completed the mission?"

"Not yet sir," they replied. They stopped before the throne and began talking to their master. "We should have the whole village within a few days sir!" said Incubus. "Good," said Lucifer. The demons Incubus and Succubus standing before their master feeling very uncomfortable, his presence overpowered them and from deep inside they began shaking with fear! "Sir!" they said. "The people of Magdala were very easy to manipulate, they were very subjective to our control."

Incubus isn't just another one of Lucifer's demons; he is the demon which takes on the male form that lies with women in order to engage in sexual activity with them. With his partner Succubus, the demon that takes on the form of a female, these two sexual demons are sent upon mankind to pollute their minds and bodies. "Sir! The town of Magdala will be under our control very soon." "Do you need any more help?" asked Lucifer. "No sir!" said Succubus. "I think we can handle this mission. We have enough men, sir."

THROUGH THE EYES OF THE ANGELS **43**

"I have ordered your servant Lilu to disturb and seduce women in their sleep, while Lilitu takes on the form of a female, appears to men in their erotic dreams. We also have Ardat Lili who visits men by night and begets ghostly children and Irdu Lili visits women by night and also begets children from them.

"Good!" replied his master Lucifer as he turned around on his chair facing his demons saying, "The mind of mankind is so weak, it will be very easy to fool them all. Incubus, I want you to take my servant Amezyarak along with you, and you report to him."

The demon Amezyarak is one of the most trusted followers of Lucifer. He loves the texture of the human skin and loves getting into the bodies of humans just for the fun of it.

Lucifer then turned towards Amezyarak and said, "I want you to take control of the town and subdue it; have total dominion over the inhabitants of this village, and from there we will move further north, as we did before and take all the cities one by one. Once this is done report back to me."

Back in the village of Magdala, the demons possessed many hosts. The people of the village began ravelling in their corruption and perversion.

"We need a host that will help us influence more people to our ways," said the demon Amezyarak.

"Yes sir!" replied Incubus, "And I think I have just the person that can do that sir."

"Who is this man?" Amezyarak asked.

"It's not a man, but a woman," said Incubus. "We've had her under our control for several years and many have been following her."

"Good," said Amezyarak. "Come my demon friends and together, let's join with this host and get her to do our bidding. For our master wants results, this town must be under our control now."

When Jesus had finished preaching in Capernaum and seeing that some of the people were trying to get to him to force him to become King, he and his disciples got in a boat and decided to go on the other side. As they cross the river, they came into the village of Magdala, it was very late. After finding a place to camp they decided to go and get some supplies in the village. So, while Jesus was resting Philip, John, James and Judas went to the village to get him something to eat.

When they got to the market of Magdala they came across a large and noisy crowd of people dancing in the street. They stopped to observe what was going on. Suddenly, the large crowd of people began dancing around in a circle surrounding the disciples.

"This must be a party or some sort of festival," said James. As they looked in the middle of the crowd there was a woman dancing going around and around in circles, dancing in the most provocative manor she came towards the disciples and began tormenting them. She put the scarf she was holding around John's neck and started playing with him trying to get him to dance with her. John managed to pull away from her and she began to laugh.

Philip came forward together with James and Judas; they tried to rebuke the demons that were standing before them, but still the woman continued to rebel and dance all around them as if they had no power or control over her. She continued to dance into the night, and slowly went back dancing into the crowd.

James said, "What's wrong? Why didn't our words have any effect on this woman? Who is she? And what kind of demons are we dealing with? Why didn't our words have any effect upon her? Jesus gave us power to cast out demons and we did the same thing in the village in Jerusalem, so why doesn't it work now?"

After the music had finished, she came back to Philip and the other disciples and said to them, "I see you are strangers in the village, where did you all come from?"
"Across the river and while our master is resting, we have come here to get some food," said John.
The woman looked deep into Philip's eyes and with a seductive look, said to him, "Do you like what you see? I know that you want me."
Again Philip said to the woman, "I rebuke that spirit and I command you to come out of her."
She said. "You foolish boy, how dare you come into my village talking to me like that? Don't you know who I am? I have men begging at my feet. This village is under my control; all these people belong to me. So, if you are not going to join us, I suggest that you finish what you're doing and get out of here."

Again, she began dancing around and around and went back to join the crowd of people dancing and laughing throughout the night. The disciples, realising that their words had no effect on this woman, left, went to get their food and returned to meet Jesus.

Making their way back to the camp, still trying to comprehend what happened, why couldn't they cast out the demons from that woman! When they got to Jesus he was sitting around the fire in deep conversation with the rest of his disciples.

John spoke first and said, "Master, something strange happened while we were in the village tonight."

"Yes," said Philip, James and Judas.

John continued, "When we arrived in the village to get the supplies we encountered some of the people in the market dancing and ravelling-"

"But it didn't feel right," said Philip. "The atmosphere felt cold and horrible, it was as if these people were possessed and then this woman tried to seduce us, it seemed that she had the whole village under her control."

Jesus began to explain to the disciples about God's Kingdom and the kingdom of darkness. They all sat and listened and the conversation went on late throughout the night.

In the morning Jesus and his disciples got ready to go back to Capernaum.

But Jesus said to Philip, "Let's go to the market."

Philip replied, "But Lord, we don't need anything."

Jesus said to him, "While it is still daylight, I have to do the work of my father who sent me, a daughter of Abraham needs us."

As they entered the market the people looked at them knowing that they were strangers and that they did not belong here.

As they moved through the market, again the woman appeared from a shop and began walking towards Jesus. As she got closer this voice came from deep down from inside her, she shouted, "What have we to do with you Jesus of Nazareth, son of the Most High God?"

Jesus shouted, "Shut up and come out of her you unclean spirits, all of you, come out now."

And in an instant, she fell to the ground tossing and turning, and all the demons left her, all seven of them. Jesus commands his disciples to help her up and bring her to him. They carried her to him. The woman, feeling weak and unable to speak, stood before Jesus with her head looking down on the floor too ashamed to look him in the eye.

"Thank you Master," she said.

Her voice was low, it was difficult to hear what she was saying. Jesus put his hand under her chin to see her face; he looked deep into her very soul and asked, "What is your name?"

She tried to master all her strength and said, "MARY, Mary Magdalene."

Then Jesus said to her, "Mary, you are now set free, go and sin no more."

Making their way back to Capernaum. The disciples asked Jesus a question. "Master, why couldn't we cast the demons out of this woman?"

He looked at them all and said, "With these kinds of demons, you need much prayer and fasting before you try to cast them out. Now let us go..."

Demons From The Gerasenes

There have been some rumours in the town about a man that is shaking Lucifer's kingdom. He is casting out his demons, healing the sick and raising the dead. The news has gotten to the ears of Lucifer. So, he summoned his most evil warriors together. First, he summoned the demons Incubus and Succubus. These two wicked demons were the ones that plagued the minds and bodies of mankind, in the cities of Sodom and Gomorrah and its surrounding towns. They came under God's judgment, which was to destroy the city, and its corrupt inhabitants that gave themselves up to sexual immorality and perversion.

He also summoned a group of young demons numbering about one hundred. These were the ones in days of old, the ones who decided to leave their home in the Celestial City. They decided to come to the inhabitants of the earth and fell in love with the daughters of men, which was forbidden by the Most High. The women had children from these angels and because of their interbreeding, some of their offspring became giants. These angels taught the inhabitants of the earth secrets of things pertaining to heaven. These are some of the leaders that was in charge.

Azazel - He taught men to make swords, daggers, shields, and breastplates. He also showed them the art of making bracelets and ornaments.

Zaqiel - He taught the art of make-up by beautifying the eyes and eyelids, the most precious stones and all kinds of coloured dyes.

Amezarak - He taught all those who cast spells and cut roots.

Armaros - He taught the release of spells.

Baraqiel - He taught astrologers.

Kokabiel - He taught portents.

Tamiel - taught astrology, and

Asradel - He taught the path of the Moon.

They became some of the most evil spirits to ever set foot on this earth. They were the ones in the time of Noah, the ones that caused the God of heaven to destroy mankind with a flood.

THROUGH THE EYES OF THE ANGELS

Lucifer addresses them all. "I have summoned you all together because of the news that I have been hearing. What is going on?" He shouted! "Why are my soldiers dropping their swords?" Kokabiel came forward; "Master," he said, "a Legion of our followers just returned back to the lair."

"What do you mean?" asked Lucifer. "There is a man by the name of Jes-Jesu-" It was as if the word would not come out of his mouth. "Speak up you fool," shouted Lucifer. "His name is Jes-Jesus – who entered into the region of the Gerasenes, where your servants had hold of this host for several years. They controlled him and told him what to do. But this morning, this man met the host and ordered your entire legion to come out of him. This is a mere mortal, how could he do this?" Turiel said! "He was going to send them back to the Abyss, but they begged him to send them into a heard of pigs and he gave them permission. But the pigs did not make a good host, so they all went over a cliff and killed themselves; and now all your servants have returned here. The whole town is talking about this man."

Lucifer's fury got the better of him and he shouted, "Who is this man that they called Jesus who has so much power in his hands?"

THROUGH THE EYES OF THE ANGELS **53**

"We don't know master!" He shouted again as he slams his fist on the table, "Who is this man that they call Jesus who heals the sick and raised the dead? Who, at the mere mention of his name, my foot soldiers drop their swords and they can't even utter his name?"

"Master! Some say Elijah has come again," a demon said, "some say he's an angel that has come to dwell with man."

Lucifer asked, "Where is this man now?"

"All the people were fearful of what he did in that region and they asked him to leave town, sir."

"Come closer my faithful servants, I know I can depend on you," said Lucifer! "I think this is the man I met in the wilderness, that desolate place. I challenged him but he managed to resist me. He seemed to be strong and he also had two of Michael's men, Raguel and Raphael looking after him. I know that he cannot be the messiah. I made sure that we killed the promised child when we got Herod to kill all those children. So, who is this man? We know that he hears from the God above. We know that the God of heaven has allowed him to see into our world. But remember that he is just a man – Yes, a mere mortal. I have killed thousands of prophets before him and he will be no different."

Lucifer called on three of his warriors, "Asael, Armaros, Ananel, I want you three to get into the priests and leaders. Urakiba and Ramiel, I want you two to get to the people, turn them against this Jesus and get them to kill him! And when he is dead and his soul is in my prison – we will see who is God! Now go. And do not stop until this man is dead!"

Baraqiel, a treacherous and evil spirit who knows how to corrupt mankind, said to his master, "Master! This man has twelve followers; there must be one of them I could reach."

"Yes," said his master, "that's a good idea! Find out which one is weak and seduce him, so that we can use him later."

THROUGH THE EYES OF THE

ANGELS

Demons' Plan

Somewhere deep in the dungeon, Baraqiel has gathered together some of his fellow demons for help. "As you've all heard, the master has given me the authority to find a way to get to that Jesus. The friends that he has following him, we need a strategy on how to get to them. Samsiel, Turiel - I want you to find out who they all are. Asael - once we know who they are, I want you to find all their old friends, anyone that knows these men. We must be able to find one that we can influence and use. Everyone has a past; every man has something that he doesn't want someone else to know about, yes? Mankind is full of secrets and that's what we will use to destroy him. Yes, his secrets. Now go my friends and find them."

A few days went by and Samsiel, Turiel and Asael the demons, once again gathered in the dungeon to discuss their findings. "Well!" said Baraqiel "What did you all find out?"

"Sir! I followed three of this man's followers, John, Philip and Matthew; I followed them, trying to stay as close to them as possible. But I found nothing that we could hold them with. I thought that Matthew the tax collector would be an easy target, but in his heart, he is a righteous man."

"Me too," said Turiel. "I too could not find anything that I could accuse them of. I followed my three but I thought I had something on one of them, the one called Peter. I thought because he had a wife, I could break him if I get to her. So, I made her very sick with a fever and she should have died, but that man – his Master, he came and told the sickness to leave and it left her."

"That man is becoming a big problem to us. We need to get rid of him now!" he shouted. "Who else?" He looked towards Asael. "And you, Yes?"

"The three who I was following – they all stood up to the test. And I was about to give up hope that we could find anything that we could hold these men with while they were around this Jesus, but I was discussing it with Zaqiel and we all know that he loves a good gossip. He told me that the one they called Judas has a history, before he met this Jesus. He used to hang around with some friends; some of them are now leaders in the temple."

"Good!" said Baraqiel.

"So, I got words to some of our followers underground and got them to find those so call friends of that Judas. It turns out that he's old friend, this Benjamin, has been under our control anyway. Ignatius has been suppressing him for many years."

"At last we're getting somewhere. Summon Ignatius to me NOW!"

Ignatius enters into the dungeon – with a very uncomfortable look upon his face. Thinking, why am I here? I must be in trouble with Baraqiel. I know how wicked he is, what have I done? He questioned himself as he walked into the presence of Baraqiel with fear on his face, unable to stop his body from shaking with fear...

"Ignatius, I have been told that you are holding a man by the name of Benjamin."

"Yes sir!" Still feeling very fearful.

"Well! I want you to tell me all about this man. What is his spirit?"

Oh! I'm not in trouble! Ignatius thought to himself. "Well! Yes sir," he said with a bit more confidence. He began to explain; "The spirit man that I control is one that loves to boast. He thinks that he is great, he is also a liar and a cheater, he love's money, he has a history of gambling and he owes money to many people."

"Anything else?" Baraqiel asked.

"He also has some friends in the Sanhedrin."

"Good!" said Baraqiel.

"That's all sir!" Ignatius said and a sense of relief came over him.

"Now gather round, all of you, we need to get this Benjamin to reunite with this Judas again."

Disciples Go Out

Jesus called his twelve disciples: Peter and his brother Andrew, James and his brother John, Philip and Bartholomew, Thomas and Matthew the tax collector, James, Thaddaeus, Simon the Zealot and Judas Iscariot. Again, he gave them authority to drive out impure spirits and to heal every disease and sickness. He gave them instructions: "You all go in pairs. Do not go among the Gentiles or enter any town of the Samaritans. Only go to the lost sheep of Israel. As you go, proclaim this message," he said: "'the kingdom of heaven has come near.' Heal the sick, raise the dead, and cleanse those who have leprosy, drive out demons. Freely you have received; freely you give."

Cornelius was a businessman who made his money by the misfortune of others. As a trader he deals with commodities and having such a successful business, he has made some influential friends. While Cornelius and a client were having a meeting, two strangers came knocking on the door. His servant went and answered the door. The strangers asked to see the master of the house. They were escorted to a waiting room while the servant went to get his master.

"Sir! You have two visitors waiting for you, they are in the waiting room and they want to discuss some matters with you."

"Do you know who they are?" asked his master.

"Yes, sir. They say their names are Simon the Zealot and Judas Iscariot."

His client Benjamin looked up when he heard the name.

Benjamin Radix, a corrupt individual also known to the authorities as a small-time hustler said,

"Judas Iscariot? What on earth is he doing here?"

"Do you know this man?" Cornelius asked.

"Yes, he is an old friend of mine. We did some business together. That's until he met up with this man he's been hanging around with, this so-called prophet."

"Do you know what they want?" Cornelius asked.

"No! But I've been hearing a lot about that man, the prophet he's hanging around with. It seems that this prophet might have a lot of money; they say he's very rich."

"The man has money, has he?" Cornelius said. "Maybe I need to get to know this man. Come join us, this could be very interesting," said Cornelius to Benjamin, as they both walked towards the waiting room.

On entering the waiting room, Cornelius greeted the two strangers.

"Good evening, my name is Simon, and this is Judas."

"Welcome, I am Cornelius, and this is a colleague of mine -" Before Cornelius could finish his sentence, Benjamin said, "Judas, it is you," and he greeted Judas with a hug like old friends. "It's good to see you again."

"Yes," said Judas. "Let's catch up, lots to talk about," Benjamin said.

After their greetings, Cornelius said, "It's a small world, I believe you and Benjamin's friendship goes way back."

"Yes!" said Judas.

"Anyway, how can I help you?" asked Benjamin. Simon began to speak to Cornelius and Benjamin. "As you may or may not know, we are the disciples of the man they called Jesus. We come to show you that our Scriptures had foretold of his coming.

Cornelius abruptly interrupted Simon; "Don't tell me you're coming here to try to convince me to become one of his followers. Look, don't get me wrong," said Cornelius, "I am a God-fearing man, but I live by this motto, 'live and let live'. I have a successful business and I try to do the best that I can. I try to uphold our religious laws and beliefs. Yes, the man you call Jesus could be a prophet, but my life is good, I can't leave all this and follow him."

Judas said, "We are not asking you to follow Him. But He is here to show us what God wants and expects from us."

Just then Benjamin interrupted, "Judas, I know you, we go way back, how can you just give up everything and follow that prophet? How are you managing for food, for money? Can this man supply all your needs? You have a brain for heaven's sake man, you're an accountant, wake-up!"

Judas began to explain to them both, "Yes! I know it's hard to believe but He is more than a man. He moves and works in the power of God. I've seen many of his miracles, and his words are not like any man's I've ever heard. I think that He is the Messiah we have been waiting for."

The four men continued their discussion late into the evening.

"I would like to meet this man," Cornelius said, "he sounds like a man after my own heart."

Cornelius smiled at Simon and Judas, as the thought went through his mind.

"The Scriptures did say that when the messiah comes, he would restore Israel back to this people. Maybe we could do some business together; maybe I can help Him to become King if He is supposed to rule Israel."

Simon, sensing that it is getting very late and that it will take more than this meeting to convince this man, Cornelius, he stood up.

"We have enjoyed meeting you both, but the time has passed us and we should be making way."

They both began to shake Cornelius and Benjamin's hands.

"I bid you goodnight and I would like if you can arrange a meeting so I can meet your teacher please," said Cornelius. "Judas," said Benjamin, "we will catch up soon."

Making their way back to the others, Judas and Simon got into conversation about the evening.

"It's been quite an evening," said Judas, "imagine bumping into my old friend Benjamin."

"Yes," said Simon. "it seems that they're both unusual characters – How did you meet Benjamin?"

"He is someone from my past. Someone I'd rather like to forget."

All the disciples got back to Jesus, they were very excited that by their hands, they did all kind of miracles.

A few days later, Judas came to the market with Andrew and John to buy some food as their supplies were running low. Judas, being an accountant, was given the duty of being in charge of the moneybag, and so when supplies were required, he was the one who would pay for it and reported back to Jesus on his expenditures. Coming out of a grocery store the three disciples bumped into Judas' old friend, Benjamin.

"Hello Judas," said Benjamin, "fancy bumping into you again."

"It's been nearly three years since we last saw each other and now, within a few days, we've seen each other twice. Let's have a drink, you and your friends." Judas looked at Andrew and John as if to say - yes! But John said, "Look, it's okay, you and your friend go, Andrew and I will take these supplies back to camp."

"Don't stay out too late and don't get drunk," Andrews said laughingly.

The two disciples left Judas and Benjamin and made their way back to camp.

Making their way to the inn, Benjamin put his arms around Judas's shoulder.

"It's good to see you again old friend, it's been too long."

"What have you been up to?" asked Judas.

"This and that," answered Benjamin, "you know what it's like."

"What's the deal with you and Cornelius?" Judas asked.

"He is filthy rich and I am trying to get him to invest in this new venture," said Benjamin. "What venture?"

"Sorry mate can't tell you; secret stuff. I can't tell you about it unless you want a piece of the action."

Judas just laughed, "Sorry my lifestyle has change now – ever since I met Jesus, He's change me completely."

"Judas, that's fine but think about this, when I do this deal, you will make at least ten thousand shekels, and with that sort of money, you never have to work again, not ever! And besides, you can still follow that Jesus if you wish," Benjamin said. "We've always talked about 'the big pay-out' that we hoped would come our way one day. Think now Judas this is the moment. This will change your whole life, I promise."

"The evening went very well, tonight was great," Benjamin said. "I really think that fate has got us together again, Judas. Look, think about what I've said, you can't go wrong with this deal, no one will get hurt. Just think, you'll have all that money and you can still follow that prophet, Jesus; what else do you want?"

Judas looked at Benjamin, "Yes! It was good catching up with you again. But as for this deal I am not sure – it's not me anymore. I am a different person now!"

"Judas, look, just give it a few days and think about it."

"Okay!" Judas said. "Now I really must go, the others will be wondering where I am."

The two said their goodbyes and went their separate ways. But as Judas made his way back to the other disciples, the thought pondered in his mind.

Back in the palace dungeon, Ignatius made his way to report back to Baraqiel. I think captain Baraqiel will be very pleased with what I have to say to him. As Ignatius entered the room to see captain Baraqiel his heart began beating a little faster. "Ignatius!" shouted Baraqiel, "I hope you have some good news for me."

"Yes, captain I have. I manage to get Benjamin and this crooked businessman together, and they had a meeting with Judas and another one of the disciples. And today Judas and Benjamin met up again."

"That's great," said Baraqiel. "You've done well!"

"But that is not all, sir," he said. "That man they call Jesus, I just heard from our spies that he has a good friend by the name of Lazarus. Sir!" Ignatius continued, "Maybe we can use this Lazarus to get to that Jesus."

"Yes! Use anything and everyone we have to get him. We cannot rest, you know our master don't like excuses." Baraqiel stood there for a moment thinking, then he said, "Yes! I want you to set up a business deal with this Cornelius and that Benjamin. Which one of our soldiers is assigned to Cornelius?"

"Envy has been suppressing him for some time now!"

"And about this Jesus; they say he has lots of money."

"Yes, sir!"

"Make Cornelius use this Benjamin to arrange a meeting with this Jesus," Baraqiel said. "Now, go and get Envy and carry out my bidding."

And with that, Ignatius made his exit with the feeling of self-achievement upon his face.

THROUGH THE EYES OF THE ANGELS

Ignatius called a secret meeting between himself and Aegrotos the demon behind all plagues. He takes great pleasure in inflecting his disease on mankind. The two demons met in a corner within the palace dungeon. "Aegrotos, I need you to do a job for me, it is very important, and you will be greatly rewarded," said Ignatius. "You see, I have to prove myself to captain Baraqiel."

The two sat down as Ignatius explain to Aegrotos his mission.

"I want you to attack a host. I want him dead, and I want it done quickly. I have spoken to Death and he is waiting on you. In fact, we all depend on you. There is a man by the name of Lazarus, we need you to get to him. We have been ordered to destroy the man they called Jesus. It will hurt him very much if we kill his best friend, Lazarus. Now go – and remember this is an urgent job."

"Yes sir!" Aegrotos said.

"And report back to me as soon as it is done."

THROUGH THE EYES OF THE ANGELS **69**

The Death Of Lazarus

While Jesus was away in a different town, his friend Lazarus became very sick. He had a sister called Mary, she was the one who poured perfume on the Lord and wiped His feet with her hair. When her brother got sick she sent word to Jesus. But He did not come. By the time Jesus came to see Lazarus he had already been dead for four days. Martha, knowing the law, knew that after four days her brother's body was decomposed and there was nothing anyone could do.

Many friends came to Martha and Mary to comfort them for the loss of their brother Lazarus. When Martha heard that Jesus was coming, she went out to meet him,

"Lord," Martha said, "if you had been here, my brother would not have died. But I know that even now God will give you whatever you ask."

Jesus said to her, "Martha, your brother will rise again." Martha answered, "I know he will rise again in the resurrection at the last day."

Jesus said to her, "I am the resurrection and the life. The one who believes in me will live, even though they die."

Ignatius once again met up with Aegrotos. "I want to thank you for all that you have done, the master is very please."

"It was quick and the job was well executed. Lazarus has been dead for four days now." "And big D! I like to call him that," smiled Ignatius. "Death has him all locked up. It's great when a plan comes together."

"Yes, another one for the master."

Just then demons from every corner of the dungeon came out shouting, running and screaming saying,

"He's gone, he's gone," as they rush towards the inner circle – the throne room of Lucifer.

Ignatius stopped one of the demons running down the corridor.

"What is happening? What is all the commotion?" He asked.

"Hurry! Hurry! It's impossible! It's impossible!"

"What? Shouted Ignatius!

"He's gone. He's gone." the demon said as he ran passed Aegrotos and Ignatius.

"Let's go and see what's happening."

The demons hurried to the throne room. As they entered, the smell of fear filled the atmosphere, they were all afraid; fear and trembling seized them all. With the look of terror on their faces, Ignatius thought to himself, what is happening? As he looked up, he saw the hands of Lucifer around the neck of Death!

"Now speak to me you little earth worm!" said his master. "For thousands of years I have ruled this earth. Even before mankind was upon it – it was mine… Never! Never! Never before has anyone broken out of my prison after four days! How dare you come to me telling me that a prisoner has gone? Where can he go?" Asked Lucifer looking at Death with such evil look that send shivers down the back of all his demons. And in a rage of anger he threw Death across the room. As Death tried to stand up, trying to compose himself, Lucifer moved back and sat down. The hall was quiet and for a moment, not a sound could be heard. Lucifer calmed himself.

"Now you insignificant fool, tell me exactly what happened." Death stood up, trying to compose himself. He began to explain.

"Master," he said, "this soul has been dead for three days, and we all know the law that on the fourth day there is no going back. It is impossible; a soul cannot go back to the human world. It has no body to occupy; his old vessel has gone into decay – so there is no going back."

Death continued, "Today, while I was guarding the prisoners, I heard this voice –" "Whose voice?" his master asked.

"I don't know sir," he said. "The voice shouted, 'Lazarus come out.' It shook the whole foundation of the prison, and I saw something that I have never seen before – Master! With my own eyes - I saw this soul walked out through the gates. I saw the flesh began to wrap itself around him and then he just vanished."

"Why didn't you try to stop him?"

"Master! I could not move, it was like the voice – Well!" Unable to say what he means as if he was confused. "Master, it sounded just like the beginning! Impossible!"

As if Lucifer knew what Death was trying to say, "Impossible! Impossible! Impossible I say!" He shouted.

"How dare He! How dare He. He knows the law – and now He has decided to break it. He has given too much power to that man, Jesus."

He then shouted, "That's enough! This man must die. We MUST kill this man. NOW!"

THROUGH THE EYES OF THE

ANGELS

Feeding The Five Thousand

The day came, Jesus went up on a mountainside and sat down with his disciples. The Jewish Passover Festival was near. When Jesus looked up, He saw a great crowd of people coming towards him. He began to talk to them, teaching them about the kingdom of God. After a while the people were hungry, He saw a boy with five loaves and two small fishes.

Jesus said to his disciples, "Make the people sit down." There was plenty of grass in that place and they sat down; about five thousand men were there. Jesus then took the loaves and fishes from the boy gave thanks and distributed to those who were seated, and they all ate as much as they wanted.

When they had all had enough to eat, He said to his disciples,

"Gather the pieces that are left over, let nothing go to waste."

When all the people saw the miracle that Jesus performed, they began to say, "Surely this is the Prophet who is to come into the world". And some of them began saying; "this must be the one that is to be the new King of Israel, the one the Scriptures spoke about." But Jesus, knowing that they intended to come and make him King by force, left them and went to another mountain by himself.

Sitting in the crowd was Benjamin; while everyone was eating, he went up to Judas. "What are you doing here?" asked Judas. "I had to see you today about that business deal we spoke about. There have been great developments. I heard that your teacher was teaching here today, so I knew that you would be here. So here I am," said Benjamin. "It's true, this could be the King of Israel, from what I've just seen, He's truly moving under the power of God."

"Judas, if you want in with this deal, we need to put down some investment. We have to pay our supplier upfront for the first shipment. I'm meeting up with the man in the market in the next few days, do you have any money?"
"No!" said Judas!

"So, what are we going to do?" ask Benjamin? "Isn't there any way you can get some money?" Judas reply, "I don't think so, not at this short notice." "But Judas, you're the man that looks after the money for that Jesus, you're in charge of the purse, man! You can easily borrow the money and put it back once the deal has gone through and no one will be any wiser, you're the accountant man! Come on Judas. I know you; you know that this is a good deal. Just like old times."

"Yes, I know, that is the problem," said Judas, "it's just like old times... Let me think about it."

"NO! We're out of time," replied Benjamin, "I need to know now, we need the cash to give the man tomorrow, otherwise the deal is off; and we all lose. I see that you have the purse with you – what is the problem? The deal is good to go," said Benjamin.

"In two days' time we will have our first order. Now are you in or out, Judas?"

Judas replied, "I would like to talk about it, but I am very busy can't talk at the moment. Maybe we meet up later?"

"Okay!" replied Benjamin. We can meet up at Cornelius' house around eight thirty tomorrow evening."

"Yes, okay," said Judas, "but now I have to get back to work, helping to serve this crowd."

That evening Benjamin went to see Cornelius.

"I was with Judas today down the Northern Valley where his master was teaching. I believe that this Jesus is who they say He is." Benjamin said to Cornelius. "I saw this man feed thousands of people today; He had nothing more than two fishes and five loaves of bread."

"Did you really see that?" ask Cornelius.

"Yes, I did! It was truly a miracle."

"That's great," said Cornelius, "it seems the Scriptures were right. Look Benjamin, a few of my associates are talking about this Jesus; it looks like He is really making a name for Himself. There are mixed feelings about Him. Some wants to make Him King and others hate Him and want Him dead. Because He is making Himself equal to God, saying that He is the Son of God. Whatever or whoever He is, this is our chance to get rich." Benjamin looked a bit confused!

"What do you mean?" he asked.

"Look Benjamin! You must stop thinking so small. Here is an opportunity that could make you and I very powerful and have great influence." Cornelius said, "Can you imagine if we were the ones behind getting this Jesus to rule Israel? If He is truly the Messiah as the Scriptures says, this Jesus will be so grateful knowing that we helped Him; our reward will be great! That's what we have to do and we have an ace card – Judas! He is close to that man. He can help convince Jesus that this is the right time — the Romans have been ruling over us for far too long. The people are crying out for a leader, a new King. Remember, God used Moses and he overthrew the Egyptians. I think the same thing can happen here. Remember, Scriptures do not lie. 'But you, Bethlehem, in the land of Judah, are by no means least among the rulers of Judah; for out of you will come a ruler who will shepherd my people Israel.' Benjamin, this is it, I can feel it in my bones. But we must come with a plan; we have to be very careful with Judas, he must never suspect what we are doing."

"Leave Judas to me," said Benjamin, "I have an idea."

"Good," said Cornelius.

THROUGH THE EYES OF THE

Plans To Make Him King

Judas met up with Benjamin and Cornelius.

"Welcome sir," said the servant. "Judas, the master is expecting you. They are in the dining room."

The servant led the way with Judas following him. Judas entered the room. Benjamin and Cornelius greeted Judas.

"How are you doing Judas?" said Cornelius, "Can I get you something to eat or drink?" "Just a drink," answered Judas.

"Sit down man and have dinner with us," Benjamin insisted that Judas sit down at the dinner table.

"Just help yourself," said Cornelius. And as they sat down Cornelius asked Judas about himself, how comes he's now following that Jesus.

"You see! I didn't pick him. He picked me. I was at a point in my life where I wasn't sure what to do," said Judas. "I wanted a change; I hated living like I was nothing and with Rome always on your back wanting you to conform. I prayed that our people would be delivered from this oppression. The Romans have been suppressing us for far too long. So, when Jesus came along, he gave me hope."

"Judas let me get straight to the point," said Cornelius, "I have many friends, powerful people in high places, leaders that think the same way; your teacher Jesus, He is what we need now, Israel needs Him. We can help Him if He is who you say He is – there are enough of us to challenge the Roman Empire. And if God is on our side, how can we lose?"

The three men carried on talking for some time... It was like they were thinking the same thing.

"Selling arms to the Romans that's nothing, but if you can see the big picture we can become rulers."

"Yes! But if we can help Jesus get into power, do you know how rich and powerful you can be?"

"This has been a long time coming, you see I hate the Romans as much as anyone, but there's a right way and a wrong way of doing things. If we try to over thrown the Romans there will be too much bloodshed. The right way is to make this Jesus the King of Israel and then we slowly take over."

Judas replied, "Somehow, I can not see Jesus being force to become king."

"Yes I understand," said Cornelius, "but if His hand was forced, I don't think He'll have a choice. Anyway, enough about Jesus; Judas, we have to focus on the immediate goal. In just two days time we have our first shipment of merchandise, is everything ready?" Asked Cornelius as he turned around, looking at Benjamin.

"Yes! Everything is ready, only one little problem."

"And what's that?" asked Cornelius.

"The matter of money."

"What money? I thought that was taken care of."

"Yes! Most of it has, it's just that Judas still needs to put in his share of the investment."

Cornelius looked at Judas with a slight look of surprised on his face and asks him, "Is there a problem Judas?" he asked.

"No! I have my share with me."

"Well done my friend," said Benjamin as he slapped his hand upon the shoulders of Judas as a gesture of congratulations. With his hands on Judas' shoulders, Benjamin asks him, "How did you do it my friend? How did you get the money? I thought we were going to do this without you."

"No," said Judas! "I didn't have the money - but you were right! This was a good deal and a big chance, we will make lots of money. So, I have borrowed the money and I'll put it back once we get rid of our first shipment."

As Judas finished speaking, Cornelius lifted his glass and said, "here's to a prosperous relationship."

After their meal Judas said his goodbyes. As he left Cornelius' house a sense of achievement came over him. The thought pondered through his mind. At last, he said to himself, my days of worrying about money could be over and a smile came over his face as he made his way back to the camp, where the other disciples was sitting around the fire, talking to Jesus.

ANGELS

The Pool Of Bethesda

The Archangel Michael summons the angel Phanuel. "With all that's going on, we still need to continue our daily tasks until the Lord returns," he said. "I need you to go to earth today and in Jerusalem by the sheep market, there is a pool which is called the pool of Bethesda which has five porches. There, you will find a great multitude of impotent people, from the blind, to the withered. I need you to stir up the water, and when you do, by the power of God whosoever gets in first after you have stirred it, that person will be made whole from whatsoever disease they had. Upon your return, I need you to assist the angel Zotiel in completing the designs and arrangement of the place which was created for the spirits, so that the souls of the dead might be gathered into them." Yes sir! Replied the angel Phanuel I shall leave right away.

There was a man that had an infirmity for thirty-eight years. When Jesus saw him lying there and knew that he had been in that state for a long time, he asked him, "Do you want to be made whole?"

The impotent man answered Him, "Sir, I have no one to help me to get into the pool when the water is troubled and whenever I try to get into the water, someone else gets there before me." Jesus said to him, "Rise, take up your bed, and walk." And immediately the man was made whole, and took up his bed, and walked. Jesus did that on the Sabbath and it was against the law to carry anything on that day. The Jews said to the man, "Why are you carrying your bed? It is against the law to do so on the Sabbath."

He answered them, "A man healed me and he told me to pick up my bed and walk." They asked him, "What man told you to do that?"

"I don't know who the man was." Afterward, Jesus met the same man in the temple and said to him, "You've been made whole: sin no more, or something worse will happen to you." The man went and told the Jews that it was Jesus who had made him whole. And so, the Jews persecute Jesus and tried to kill him, because he had done these things on the Sabbath day.

THROUGH THE EYES OF THE
ANGELS

Purpose And Plan Revealed

Demetrious, a loving husband and devoted father having three children; Tabitha sixteen, Rachel who was fourteen, and Simeon his only son, was twelve years old. After his two daughters were born, he prayed earnestly to God that his next child would be a boy. And so, Simeon was born, the pride and joy of his father. Demetrious was a happy and contented man and thanked God every day for his family. But the day came two days before his sons thirteenth birthday, a fever got hold of Simeon.

"Honey! This fever doesn't look good, Simeon is not getting any better," says his mum. Demetrious with tears in his eyes says,

"I just don't know what else to do for my son. The boy is just lying down on his bed unable to fight this fever." Rachel went over to her father. Demetrious calls his other daughter over, with sadness in his voice he began explaining to them.

"Your brother is very sick; I don't think he's going to make it."

Rachel said, "Father, why, is Simeon going to die?"

Unable to answer their questions he said, "I don't know, we've done all that we can for him, only God can help us now."

Rachel and Tabitha both crying as they embrace their father, whilst their mother was crying by Simeon's bedside.

"Father, he cannot, he can't die, please father, please don't let Simeon die."

"I have sent the servant into the village to find the man they called Jesus. They say that he can heal the sick."

As evening came the boy's fever worsened. With his family at his side – they all feared the worse. Rachel, with tears running down her face, said,

"Where is Jesus?"

"I don't know..." said her father. "We have called for Him, but it looks like He's going to be too late."

"No!" shouted his wife, "Don't say that, He has to heal my Simeon; my baby! Why would God want to take my son? Why?" She shouts at her husband. "Why?"

Simeon, unable to move calls for his mother, "Mother,

hel-help me!" And then he took his last breath as his spirit left his body.

His mother grabbed hold of him as he lay on the bed and uncontrollably shook Simeon, trying to wake him up. "Simeon, speak to me!" She screams, "My baby is dead! He's dead!"

A sense of grief filled the atmosphere as the spirit of death engulfed the house. Sometime had past and Demetrious' household mourned the death of his son Simeon. Just then, a servant rushes into the house and said, "Master, master, Jesus is here! Jesus is here!" Simeon's mother, still at his bedside, saw Jesus and quickly stood up.

"Master, Why? Why couldn't you have been here much sooner? My son is dead. I prayed that you would get here on time, and if you were here, my son would not have died. But it's too late. There's nothing you can do, there's nothing anyone can do." Meanwhile, all the people were wailing and mourning for him.

"Stop wailing," Jesus said, "he is not dead but asleep." They laughed at Him, knowing that he was dead. But Jesus replied, "Woman do not cry, and do not be afraid.

Only believe, for your son is not dead but he's asleep."
Demetrious went up to Jesus, "Master, he is not moving or breathing, he has been dead for some time now."

"Demetrious, all you have to do is believe and today you will see the glory of God." Jesus said, "Please leave me alone with the boy. Please, you must trust me."
As the crowd left the room, Jesus moved over to the boy and with the angels standing beside him, said,
"Simeon, Simeon, Simeon, I say to you, Arise."
The boy coughed and very slowly he started to move.
 Jesus helped him to sit up on the bed and said to him,
"Simeon, do you know who I am?"
"Sir, I was asleep and I heard you call my name. Who are you?" he asked.
"I am Jesus and I have come to save your life. Simeon, I want to tell you a story.

"A long time ago there was a man and woman by the name of Adam and Eve. They were God's pride and joy. God gave them everything, but they still disobeyed Him. So, because of them all men must die."
Simeon shouted, "No Lord, but why?"
"Because the punishment for disobedience was death, and the price has to be paid. Someone has to pay that

price. But you see, there is no man on earth who is worthy enough to pay it. No, not one! I will take all the sins of the world upon my shoulders; and I will take the place of man."

"No Lord, no!" said Simeon.

Jesus continued, "Simeon, I am the Lamb of God that will take away the sins of the world. I am going to Jerusalem and there I will suffer many things at the hands of the elders and chief priests, I will be betrayed by my friends, and there I will give my life as a ransom and be killed."

Again, Simeon interrupted, "But why you? Why must you die?"

"So that mankind can live." said Jesus.

Simeon began to cry as Jesus puts His arms around him.

"You mean you're going to let them kill you? Who is going to make the sick people better?" he asked.

"Simeon, if I don't die mankind will be lost forever. But fear not my little one, for on the third day I will rise again, and you shall see me once more."

"Yes!"

"You Simeon shall be a witness onto me."

While Jesus was explaining His mission to Simeon,

Archangel Gabriel, and the angel Saraqael stood listening in amazement. All has now been made clear, they now understood the Lord's purpose and plan. Jesus called the family and gave the boy back to them.

"You may now enter, your son lives."

Joy and happiness filled the house, with everyone shouting,

"He's alive again, Simeon's alive again!"

Simeon's mother and father thank Jesus!

"You have given me my son back," said Demetrious as his whole house-hold shouted, "He's alive! He's alive! Simeon's alive! Glory be to the Lord our God."

Plan To Betray Jesus

Several days have gone by and the demons have orchestrated a plan to get to Judas. The demon Baraqiel called Ignatius once again.

"Sir, you summoned me?"

"Yes Ignatius," replied Baraqiel, "any news on our situation with Benjamin?"

"Yes sir! We managed to get him working with Judas again. And we managed to force Judas to steal some money from his Master to invest in this deal selling weapons to the Romans. A deal that seemed too good to be true, he believed that this was the deal that was going to make him very rich."

"Good!" replied Baraqiel.

"I influenced and convince Benjamin to double cross him. So, Judas has lost all his investments."

Baraqiel just sat there in front of Ignatius and kept on nodding his head.

"Turiel has influence the leaders from the Sanhedrin that they need to get rid of Jesus quickly."

A smile came over the face of Baraqiel.

"Good," he said, "you have done well, we will make a captain out of you yet!"

"Thank you, sir!" said Ignatius as he smiles to himself. "Now get Asael and Samsiel, I want them to get to the leaders and that Cornelius to work together to get to this Jesus. Don't take any chances, pull out all the stops, we need this man now! Our master is getting very impatient, we must move fast."

Ignatius bowed before Baraqiel and slowly moving backwards, he left, grinning to himself thinking how proud he was.

Standing in front of the house of Cornelius the businessman, a man stood knocking the door. The servant of the household answered and invited the man in, asking him to wait while he gets his master.

"Master, you have a visitor wanting to see you. He is in the waiting room."

"Do you know who this man is?" Cornelius asked.

"No Sir, but he seems to be one of the leaders from the temple."

"Okay, I'll be there in a moment."

A few moments later Cornelius made his way down-stairs to his waiting room. As he opened the door, he saw a priest from the temple sitting on his sofa drinking a glass of water.

"Good evening," he said with his hand stretched out waiting to shake his visitor's. "I am Cornelius."

"Greetings," replied the visitor, "my name is Samuel. I represent some of the leaders from the Sanhedrin. They have sent me here to ask you for help."

"How can I help the leaders of our people? Why are they coming to me? I am nothing more than a mere businessman."

"That is why they have sent me here." Samuel said. "Let me explain."

"Please do!" said Cornelius. He sat down opposite Samuel.

"Sir, you see, we know you have some influential friends in the temple. We're also aware that you are in close contact with a man that the authorities have got under investigation, the man by the name of Benjamin Radix," said Samuel. "He's been under surveillance for quite a while, but we have allowed him to operate because he is no threat to us. But recently we notice that you have had several meetings with this man."

"Yes, indeed I have." replied Cornelius. "We are in the process in doing some business together and let me tell you," said Cornelius, "this is a legitimate business."

"Oh yes, sir, we know, we are well aware of that," said Samuel. "Our interest is not with him nor yourself but the man by the name of Judas Iscariot, it is him we're interested in."

"Can I ask why?" asked Cornelius.

"From our sources we have evidence linking you all together."

"And is that a crime?" Cornelius asked.

"No, sir," replied Samuel, "that is why we have come to you. The leaders of the Sanhedrin need a very big favour from you. It is one that will be very profitable to you, sir. And being such a shrewd businessman like yourself, we believe that this offer will be more than satisfactory."

"Tell me more," said Cornelius.

"Sir, let me explain! For years we the leaders of Israel have led our people, we have kept all our traditions, our way of life. It hasn't been easy under Roman laws, but we have been living peacefully. But now we have encountered a problem, a very big problem by the name of Jesus. A man who the people thinks is a prophet. Some even believe the he is the Messiah, the one that is to come into the world and rule Israel.

"There are rumours going around that he is the King of the Jews and the worse thing being said is that he is the Son of God. Sir, can you imagine what chaos this will cause when it gets to the ears of Caesar, when he hears that there's another king in his kingdom? He will go crazy - there will be bloodshed, the Romans will come crashing down on all our heads, if the people start worshipping another king. And it is for that reason we the leaders need to get to this man, to talk to him to put a stop to all this for all our sakes."

Cornelius went quiet for a while as if in deep thought, and then he said,
"Supposing this man Jesus turns out to be who they say he is? Supposing he is a prophet, or even the Son of God? What then?"
"Sir, trust me, we the leaders are well aware of this man, we know who he is and where he came from, and I can tell you, yes, there is a slight chance he might be a prophet, because he is very knowledgeable and versed in the Scriptures. But I can assure you he is not the

Messiah much less the Son of God. He is blaspheming, making himself equal to God. This must stop! No man has the right to blaspheme our God," Samuel said with a sense of anger in his voice.

Again, the room went quiet. The two men sat opposite each other unaware that sitting beside them was Asael and Samsiel whispering in their ears, suggesting to them what to say next.

Then Samuel said, "Sir, I am not sure whether or not you believe that this man is whom they say he is. The thing we have an issue with is if the people believe that he is the Son of God, this man was born right here, we know his mother, brother and sisters. We know that his father Joseph died a few years back, so tell me, how can this man be the messiah?"

"Okay," Cornelius said, "I see your point! What can I do to help?"

"We need an inside person that is close to this Jesus and that's where you come in. Because you already have a rapport with this Judas and he trust you, we would appreciate if you could talk to him concerning this matter, explaining how it could be to his benefit and his people that Jesus come to speak to us."

Then Cornelius said to Samuel, "What is this favour worth to the Sanhedrin?"

"I have been told whatever it cost, so tell me, what's your price?"

Cornelius was lost for words. He cleared his throat as if he was caught by surprise...

At this point Asael and Samsiel smiled at each other.

"We have got him now," they said to each other.

"This man's greed has got the better of him. Now let's make him an offer he cannot refuse." Samsiel said to Asael.

"Yes! said Asael, "Humans, their minds are so weak, so easy to manipulate."

"So," Samuel said, "how about one hundred pieces of silver, is that enough for you?" Instantly, a voice went through Cornelius' mind. Do you know how long it would take you to earn one hundred pieces of silver? Man, take the money and run, he said to himself. But he tried to play it down as if he was thinking about it. He hesitated for a moment with an expression on his face as if deep in thought.

I wonder if I can push him a little more, he thought to himself. Then a smile came to his face, what the heck, he said, I have nothing to lose. So, he replied,

"Make it one hundred and fifty pieces and you got yourself a deal."

That's more money you can earn in one year, he said to himself.

Samuel stared deep into his soul, Cornelius' heart beating faster and faster, thinking, have I've pushed him too far? Then suddenly Samuel stretched out his hand to shake Cornelius' and said,

"Sir! You are a tough negotiator, but you've got yourself a deal."

Samsiel then turned to Asael, both grinning at each other and said...

"It is done! Let's go!"

Samuel and Cornelius shook each other's hand and both men felt a sense of relief as they looked into each other's eyes. Samuel said, "It was good doing business with you."

"Likewise, replied Cornelius, "the pleasure was all mine and I promise you, I will deliver that man, Jesus, to you."

Traveling deep down into the dungeon, Samsiel and Asael walked side-by-side along the dark demon infested corridor to the chamber feeling very proud of themselves, and very happy with their achievement, where their captain is waiting for news from their mission. They entered a small room where Baraqiel was waiting.

"I hope you have good news for me?" said Baraqiel.

Samsiel and Asael answered in unison, "Sir, great news, we have got Cornelius. He will help bring Jesus to the Sanhedrin where we will get them to kill him."

"Well done you two, the master will be very pleased with us."

It was the Jewish festival; the leaders, chief priest and the elders of the people came together to work out how they were going to kill Jesus. But they had to wait until after the festival so that they would not upset the people. Judas met up with Cornelius the day before the festival, and Cornelius sat him down explaining how Benjamin had double crossed them both and that he had taken the money and run.

"Yes! I know," said Judas – "I trusted him, but I should have known that he could never change."

"So, what are you going to do?" asked Cornelius.

"I don't know," said Judas. "The money was not mine; I borrowed it hoping that as soon as the deal was done,

I would put it back. But now I just don't know what to do. I am afraid that my master will find out, because I have no way of replacing it." Judas explained.

"I know," said Cornelius, "and I understand."

"You think you have everything worked out and BANG, life throws you a bad deal."

"But Judas there is still hope," Cornelius continued, "I have some good news; I have a way you can get that money back and much more."

"Please Cornelius, do not tease me," said Judas. "No!"

"Judas, I know some people that want to have a meeting with Jesus, but your master will not talk to them. From my contact I know that they will be willing to give money if you can get Jesus to just talk to them."

"How much?" asked Judas.

"I'm not sure, but I know that these leaders are desperate, they will pay you handsomely, enough to pay off all your debt and much more."

Judas' face lit up while Cornelius was talking to him, "How could I meet these people?" He said.

"That's not a problem," said Cornelius. "Go to the high priest Caiaphas and tell him that I sent you and all will be fine." Judas was so happy; he shook Cornelius' hand and thanked him for the information.

Soon, he arrived at the house of Caiaphas; the servant came and answered the door. "Can I help you sir?" He asked.

 "I have come to see the high priest, Caiaphas, a matter of great importance," Judas answered.

The servant asks Judas to wait while he goes and call the master of the house. The high priest Caiaphas entered the room. The two men shook hands and Judas said, "I was sent by Cornelius and I maybe able to help you have a meeting with Jesus. I am Judas Iscariot, one of His disciples. If it's just a meeting you want, I can get him to meet you but it's going to cost you." "Yes!" replied the high priest Caiaphas. "This will be an important meeting, wait here while I go and get your money."

When Caiaphas left the room, Judas felt happy knowing that he can replace the money he had stolen without anyone being the wiser. The high priest Caiaphas returned with a small bag of silver.

"Here you are Judas, thirty pieces of silver and thank you for arranging this meeting." As Judas was about to leave, Caiaphas said to him, "I don't mean to sound doubtful but what if he refuses to come? What if you can't deliver him? You know we might have to take him by force."

THROUGH THE EYES OF THE ANGELS

"No!" said Judas, "I don't think it will come to that. I'm sure that He will come... After all, it's only for a meeting."

So, he bid goodnight and went back to meet the other disciples.

That evening while Jesus was resting, for most of the disciples had gone out, Judas saw the opportunity to sit and have a conversation with Him.

"Master," he said, "I believe that you're the Son of God because no man can do the things that you do, but the Scriptures say that you will be made the King of Israel. Master, it is the right time. We the people are ready to come out of the depression of those Roman rulers."

But Jesus replied to him, "Judas, the time is not now, you don't understand Scriptures." "But Master, the people believe in you, the leaders of our people want to meet you. They want to talk to you. This is the right time to show them and the world who you really are." Jesus looked at Judas and said, "Judas, my friend, the leaders of this world are blind, they have eyes, but they can't see. They have ears but cannot hear. They hate me because I tell them the truth. You see, if you are of God, you'll hear God's words, they do not hear

THROUGH THE EYES OF THE ANGELS **103**

because they're not of God. So, tell your friends I will not be meeting with them."

"Master, they just want to talk."

Judas became very frustrated knowing that he would have to give the money back and if that happens, then everyone will know he's a thief. So he pretended to understand... and said,

"Yes master!"

But in his heart, he began strategising his next move.

Celebrating The Passover

"Master, we have done your bidding. I got into the high priest, Caiaphas and made him pay Judas thirty pieces of silver just as you said, and Judas will bring that Jesus to him."

The next day, the whole army of Lucifer was summoned together in the Hollow Chamber. The chamber was filled with demons from every corner. When they were all gathered together, he bellowed,
"My faithful followers listen to me. This night will be a night to remember. Thanks to my loyal servant Baraqiel, tonight we will have this man Jesus in our hands..."

When it was evening Jesus was celebrating the Passover with his disciples. While He was eating, He suddenly said to them, "Tonight, one of you is going to betray me."

The disciples began to look worried asking Him,
"Who is it?"
He replied, "The person that dips his hand into my bowl, he is the one that will betray me."
Then Judas asked him, "Surely, you don't mean me?"
Jesus answered, "You know it is, whatever you are about to do, do it quickly."

So Judas left and went to get the leaders.

Jesus then took bread, He gave thanks, broke it and gave it to His disciples, saying,
"Take it and eat it; this represents my body."
He then took a cup, again He gave thanks and gave it to His disciples, saying,
"Drink it, all of you. This represents my blood of the covenant, which is poured for the forgiveness of sins. I will not drink it again until that day when I drink with you in my Father's Kingdom."

After they finished eating, they all went to a garden nearby called Gethsemane, to pray. He told the disciples to stay there a while and He went a bit further. And being in anguish, He prayed more earnestly and his sweat was like drops of blood falling to the ground.

The angels Gabriel and Saraqael appeared to him and strengthened him. He got up and returned back to His disciples only to find that they were all sleeping. Just as He was about to wake them up, along came Judas with a large crowd armed with swords and clubs, with legions of Lucifer's followers.

"Make sure He doesn't get away this time," said a demon.

"Oh no! Tonight, He belongs to us," replied another. Judas told the crowd, "I will identify Him with a kiss." He then approached Jesus and said to him, "Greetings, Rabbi!" and kissed him.

The arresting soldiers of the High Priest then turned Jesus over to Pilate's soldiers.

Back In The Celestial City

Along the corridor of the great mansion, far on the east side of the Celestial City of the Most High, where the glass walls laminates the light, the light that forever burns, a place where there is no day or night; there stood the angel Zotiel, one of the holy angels, the warrior that protects the holy things of God. He was the one the Lord put as guardian of the tree of life back in the Garden of Eden. This tall and majestic figure over shadows the other angels that stood around him. As one of Gabriel's general he was put in charge in his absent.

"Captain Phanuel, have you anything to report?"
"Sir, I have just returned from the earth. My assignment was to disturb the pool of Bethesda so that one can be healed from any infirmities."
"Did you see Archangel Gabriel?"

"Yes sir! He and Saraqael are with the Master. But captain, the situation in Jerusalem is very intense, sir; there are legions of demons everywhere in the town. We don't really know what is happening, why the Lord is allowing all this."

"It doesn't make any sense since our Lord's departure, but we must carry on with our duties," he said to his lieutenant, "we have an assignment to complete the work and to get this place ready."

"This place is amazing, Sir!" said the angel Phanuel. "Yes!" replied Zotiel. "This beautiful and tranquil place was created so that the spirits, the souls of the dead, might be gathered into them. And the souls of the sons of men will be gathered also. There they will wait until the Day of Judgment and until their appointed time. And likewise," said Zotiel, "see that place over there," as he pointed to his left, "that also has been created for sinners, when they die and are buried in the earth, and judgment has not come upon them during their life, here their souls will be separated until the Great Day of Judgment."

Suddenly, the sound of trumpet echoed through the city as Michael the archangel makes his entrance.
"Host of heaven, Protectors of His Majesty's throne, it

has begun! We must hurry! The enemy has aroused the people and they are about to slay the Master. We already have Saraqael and Archangel Gabriel with the Master. So, we are going only as observers, and under no circumstances are we to interfere. Only if the Master specifically requests our assistance, do we engage in warfare."

When Michael had finished, he lifted his sword together with the other angels and shouted,
"For the glory of God."
And as if in one voice all the angels replied, "And for the Lamb!"

Thirty Pieces Of Silver

While the high priest Caiaphas was having his dinner, he heard this banging on his front door.

"Whoever it is," he said to his servant, "surely seem to be in a hurry."

The servant went to the door but before he could open it halfway, the door was banged open.

"Where is your master?" Judas shouted as he pushed pass the servant only to find Caiaphas standing by the archway of the door.

"Come in Judas," he said sensing the anger in Judas. "I thought you told me that you only wanted to have a meeting and to talk to Jesus? Why have you bound Him and handed Him over to the elders and scribes and the whole council."

"Look Judas, I too don't want Jesus to die, I thought your master would see sense. But he refuses to speak or work with us. But that wasn't that bad because the council could not sentence anyone for keeping quiet, they wouldn't have anything against him, but they took Jesus away to the high priest and all the chief priests, the elders and the scribes. They asked him all kind of questions, but he still refused to answer any and then Tertullus, the high priest asked him, 'Are you the Christ, the Son of God?' and Jesus said, 'Yes I am.' At this point Judas, I could not help him. You see, as you know that is unthinkable – when the high priest heard that, he ripped off his robe, and said, 'We need no other witness. We all heard this man's blasphemy,' the whole council decision was unanimous. They all condemned him to be guilty of death."

As Caiaphas was talking, Judas felt the guilt over shadowing him, until it became too much to bare. Tears filled his eyes when he realised that it was his fault that Jesus was going to die.
"There must be something we can do!"
"No!" Caiaphas said, "It is too late, nothing can be done for him now, he has been sentenced to death."

Before Caiaphas could finish Judas felt his blood boiling, the demons, Samsiel and Asael and many others began tormenting his mind, over and over

THROUGH THE EYES OF THE ANGELS

again. He hears, it's your fault; it's your fault He is going to die. He felt as if the whole world was accusing him. The voice grabbed hold of his mind, it kept on uttering, you know what to do – Kill yourself! Kill yourself! Kill yourself! Not knowing what to do, or where to go Judas took the bag of money that he received from the high priest Caiaphas and threw it on the floor, and run out of the house, crying and sobbing. Nowhere to go and nowhere to hide, the guilt kept eating at his very soul. He found himself sitting underneath a tree in a field sobbing uncontrollably, not knowing how he got there. In his mind he kept on saying, "Forgive me Lord! Forgive me Lord. All I wanted was for you to become the King of Israel and to stop us from being under the rule of the Romans."

The voice in his ears got louder and louder, the torment got more and more intense. Unaware that he was surrounded by demons tormenting his mind, one said to him, "What are you waiting for, coward?"
Other demons shouted, "Is that all he was worth, thirty pieces of silver? Just thirty pieces of silver?"
On and on the voices went, around and around in his mind, he was unable to think, unable to concentrate. As if he had no control of his thoughts, he untied the

sash around his waist, threw it up the tree and hanged himself.

"Ignatius!" said Baraqiel, "I want to congratulate you – you and your men have done a wonderful job. I will recommended to our master that you deserve to be a captain, for you have proven beyond any shadow of doubt, that you are a loyal and faithful warrior. I understand that the man Judas, his soul is now in our prison."

"Yes sir! I'm proud to say that it was a glorious victory for us."

While Baraqiel was in conversation with Ignatius, a demon entered into the room,

"Sir, our master has summoned you; he wants to see you immediately!"

Within seconds Baraqiel was before Lucifer.

"Ha! Baraqiel, my most faithful servant, I have been hearing good things about you and your team. You have served your master well."

"Yes sir! As you ordered my lord, the man Jesus has been arrested and He has been sentenced to death."

"Good," replied Lucifer.

"Sir, and the man they called Judas, one of his followers, the one who we got to betrayed him, he too, my lord, he is now in our prison."

"Yes, my servant, that was excellent work, well done," said Lucifer.

"Sir, I did not work alone, and I would not have accomplished this without the help of your loyal and faithful servant, Ignatius," said Baraqiel.

Lucifer replied, "Summon him here, now."

Ignatius entered the throne room, his body shaking with fear and trembling as he stands in his master's presence. Lucifer looks at Baraqiel and said, "I have decided that you deserved a reward for a job well done. You have shown indeed that you're one of my most trustworthy servants."

"Thank you, sir," replied Baraqiel as he bowed his head low before his master.

"I am promoting you to one of my generals."

"And you Ignatius," said Lucifer, "you have now been promoted to captain Ignatius. Well done to both of you."

THROUGH THE EYES OF THE

Pontius Pilate

When morning came, all the chief priests and elders of
the people plotted against Jesus to put Him to death.
They had bound Him, and they led Him away and
delivered Him to Pontius Pilate, the governor.

Pontius Pilate said to Jesus: "Are You the King of the
Jews?"

"Yes, you are right," Jesus Replied.

"Tell me what is it that you have done to these people?
Do you hear how many things they testify against you?
Why do they hate you so much?"

Then Pilate said to the crowd, "What kind of crime has
this man committed to deserve the punishment of
death?"

He turned around to Jesus and said, "Will you please
answer me? Don't you know that I have the power to
release you?"

Jesus said, "You have no power over me. If I wanted to, I can call legions of my angels to set me free."

He was astonished at Jesus' answer, so he turned to the crowd and said,

"It is our custom to release one prisoner, whom do you wish me to release?"

Not wanting to kill Jesus, again he said to the crowd, "Should I release Barabbas or Jesus who is called the Christ?"

With Urakiba and Ramiel manipulating the people, urging them to set free 'Barabbas', Pilate said, "What then shall I do with Jesus who is called the Christ?"

The crowd replied, "Crucify Him!"

Pontius Pilate said, "Why? This man has done nothing wrong."

But the crowd replied, "Just crucify him!"

The angels watched helplessly as the soldiers in front and behind Jesus push Him through the crowd.

"Move along! Get out the way!" the soldier shouted. "I said stand back!"

As Jesus went through the crowd, some shouted, "Jesus we love you," while others shouted; "Crucify him, crucify him,"

"He is not the messiah, he is a fake,"

"Kill him!"

"Crucify him!"

"He thinks he is a King of Israel."

The soldiers tried to move Jesus through the thick crowd; "Make way, I said, get out of the way."

As Jesus was carrying the heavy cross, he falls to the ground. A woman runs to help him and wipes his head. "Lord! Lord! Why? How can they do this to you," she said.

"Daughter of Jerusalem, do not weep for me, but weep for yourself and for your children."

Just then the soldier pushed the woman aside. She screamed at him,

"Why are you doing this? He's done nothing to hurt you!"

The soldier looked into her eyes, "Do you want to take his place woman? – Then move!"

The woman moves sadly back into the crowd, crying for the fate of the Messiah. As they were going out, they met a man from Cyrene, named Simon and they forced him to carry the cross for Jesus to the place where He was to be crucified.

"Captain!" said Saraqael, "I cannot stand here watching these humans and demons torture our Lord like this, just give me the word."

"No! My orders are that we must not interfere no matter what." And so, they stood there helpless, unable to move, unable to fight.

They hung Jesus on a cross and put an inscription over the cross, written in Greek, Latin, and Hebrew, it read: THIS IS THE KING OF THE JEWS. He hanged there between two criminals, one on His right and one on His left.

One criminal said to Him,

"Why can't you save yourself and us?"

The other criminal said to the other one,

"Don't you fear God? We are being punished for the crimes that we committed, but this man Jesus is innocent he has done nothing wrong."

He then said to Jesus, "Lord, remember me when you come into your Kingdom."

And Jesus said to him, "I promise you, today you will be with me in paradise."

From noon until three in the afternoon darkness came over all the land. About three in the afternoon Jesus cried out in a loud voice, "My God, my God, why have you forsaken me?"

When some of those standing by heard this, they said, "He's calling Elijah." The rest said, "Now leave him alone. Let's see if Elijah comes to save him."

And when Jesus had cried out again in a loud voice, He gave up His spirit. At that moment the curtain of the temple was torn in two from top to bottom. The earth shook, the rocks split and the tombs broke open.

All the demonic forces gathered around the cross, laughing and cheering, shouting,

"He is dead, He is dead."

The angels stood ready for action, wanting to fight, wanting to attack those demons. Gabriel and Michael just stood at the foot of the cross with their swords in their hands but did nothing. All the angels stood in the form of an arch around the cross, with swords in their hands and eyes on their captain waiting for the order to attack. They were being tormented by the demons around them.

"What are you going to do now your master is dead?" The demons shouted at the angels.

A demon came towards Michael looked him in the eyes and said, "Do you want some of this?" putting his fist up in his face. But Michael said not a word... Then Gabriel spoke to Michael saying,

"Look at this crowd, mankind will never understand." "I know," said Michael! "How could they know why the Lord came low from above He came in love to give His life? And how could they understand His love for man, that God would give the perfect gift of sacrifice?"

"Yes!" replied Gabriel, "If they only knew, what happened here today." And so, they stood guarding the body until evening.

Later that evening, a rich man by the name of Joseph, a council member, a good and righteous man, he was from the city of Arimathea. He once was very sick and knew that he was going to die. But Jesus came and healed him. He went to Pilate and asked for the body of Jesus. Then he took it down, wrapped it in linen and laid it in the tomb, which he brought for himself. After they had taken the body down from the cross, and placed it in the tomb, Gabriel said to Michael,

"It is finished, I must return to the city; I will leave Saraqael in charge to watch over the Lord's body."

Deep down in the palace dungeon, legions of Lucifer's followers swarmed back to their lair, all laughing and rejoicing, celebrating that the man called Jesus was dead. When they got back, they explained to their master how glorious their victory was, not even the host of heaven could stop them.

"Good!" said Lucifer; "At last this man is dead; now I'll make him suffer, like he's never suffered before, now he'll know the true meaning of pain and death."
And throughout the night the celebration went on until early in the morning.

The Missing Souls

Early in the morning on the second day after the death of Jesus, a twisted deformed spirit with the authority for collecting the souls of men by the name of Aspeican, approached the demon Death, having a worried look upon his face.

"Sir," he said, "We have a problem; you know you put me in charge of all new arrivals?" "Yes!" answered Death.

"Well sir, I can't seem to find two of the prisoners."

"What do you mean, you can't find them? What prisoners?" asked Death?

"The ones that were crucified at Calvary sir! It doesn't make any sense; we've only received one soul."

"That's impossible, all three must be there. You need to search every cell in the prison, every corner. There is nowhere to go..." said Death.

"Should we report this to the master?"

"No!" he said, "They have to be here, all human souls have to come here, that's the law. Besides, if the master finds out, we will be banished to the utmost part of hell and I'm sure we don't want that...do we? Now go, get all the help that you need, they must be here."

The next day Lucifer summoned the demon Death, sitting on his throne with his servants tending to his needs and a sense of satisfaction and relief on his face. Death walked down the corridor – with the look of confusion and fear, he hesitated, as he got closer to the entrance to the throne room.

This is not good, he said to himself. This is not going to be a good day; I think I'd rather be dead than to face the master today. He stopped when he got to the throne room. He slowly opened the door with fear gripping every part of his body. As he entered the room, he saw his master sitting down with some demons washing his feet while others were feeding him.

"Well! Look whom we have here," said Lucifer. "Come in Death, and do not be afraid. You have done well my servant, I understand that we have killed that man they called Jesus and that you have him locked up tight in our prison."

Death opened his mouth, but only to hear nothing, he tried swallowing his saliva, but his throat was too dry. He tried once more to speak but could not stop his words from stuttering.

"Mast - mast – master, I hate to be a bearer of bad news."

At this point Lucifer shouted, "STOP!" His voice echoed through the chamber and beyond the hallways of the dungeon. The demons that were attending to him suddenly stood still.

Lucifer sat up straight, Death felt as if his whole being was frozen – he could not feel his legs; all he could hear was the pumping of blood rushing to his head. Lucifer looked straight into his very soul and said,

"Bad news! What bad news? Is that man Jesus dead or not? Did we not kill him? Was he not hung on that cross?"

"Yess Sir, all what you say is true," Death answered still shaking with fear. "So, what do you mean by bad news? I don't do bad news. Come closer," Lucifer commanded Death. "Explain yourself! Explain, now!"

"Master, it is true that this Jesus hung on a cross, it is also true that he died, I was there, I saw it with my own eyes. But master, I can't find him. I saw his spirit left his body, but he's nowhere to be found."

With rage of anger in his voice Lucifer shouted, "What do you mean you can't find him? Is not his body still in the tomb?" asked Lucifer.

"No sir, we check this morning we just can't find it, it's as if he has just vanished."

As the demon Death uttered the word vanished, the whole dungeon began to rumble as if an earthquake has been unleashed. The walls began to crack, demons falling over, Lucifer trying to steady himself from falling as he grabbed hold of the table in the middle of the throne room. He shouted!

"What the HELL is going on?"

Just then the door of the throne room exploded and came crashing upon one of the demons that was in the room.

A bright light penetrated and filled the whole dungeon. Every corner, every room, every demon with their hearts pounding, trembling with fear. Death tried standing but fear tortured his guts, it overwhelmed his whole body. Demons from the four corners of the dungeon fleeing for their lives. As the light got brighter and brighter it began to move towards the centre of the throne room. All the demons were unable to look upon the light, for its brightness was brighter than that of the sun.

Lucifer tried to get back upon his throne, he clenched his fists as he hesitantly took each step and with all his strength trying to see the source of this unusual light. As he began to focus his eyes, he saw the shape of a man walking towards him.

"Who are you?" he shouted. He heard nothing. Again, he shouted, "Who are you?"

Just then the silhouette of a man walking towards Lucifer, stretched out his hands.

Again, Lucifer cried out, "Who are you?" Still trying to focus on the figure standing in front of him. Then he heard the voice, the voice that he had heard all his life since the foundation of the world.

"No! That cannot be!" he cried.

Suddenly, the voice said, "I AM the Lamb of God that has come to takeaway the sins of the world. I AM, the seed of the woman, I AM the everlasting Father."

With a deep groan as if coming from deepest part of Lucifer's belly, he shouted,

"No-o-o-o-o! How can that be? You're a man. How can you be Father?"

Holding his hands over his head as he fell to his knees. Jesus said to him, "All power has been given to me on the earth and in heaven. And now the debt has been paid, in full."

When Lucifer saw Jesus and realised that it was none other than his FATHER in the form of man, he could not contain his rage, the anger consumed him. He shouted,

"You tricked me, you lied, I hate and despise you, how dare you break the law and come to help mankind. Have you forgotten that man gave it to me back in the Garden of Eden, it's mine, I know my rights!" But Jesus said to him, "It is finished! Man is now free from death. You have no hold over him anymore." He is now free.

Yes! You may know your rights. Said Jesus - but the LAW says that if an innocent man takes the place of a guilty man who has committed a crime. Then that man who was guilty is free to go. Someone else has paid his debt. I AM that lamb that has come to take the place of man and pay his debt.
Then Jesus turned around and he walked back into the light.

Lucifer shouted, "NO! Don't you turn your back on me! This is far from finished. It's your fault! It's 'ALL' your fault! – You just want all the glory for yourself! Why? Why should everyone worship you? Why should I worship you? I will never bow down and worship you! - Am I not greater than man? Don't I deserve to be worshiped too? I know you favour mankind but they will never follow you. I am going to make sure that they all hate you. They all will come down to hell with me. Your precious man! Just like I deceived Eve and Adam I will deceive mankind again they are weak and foolish, and with my followers we will get them all. As long as I live, I promise, I will kill them, I will destroy them all!"

The Resurrection

It was the day of preparation for the Sabbath, which was dawning. The women who came with Jesus from Galilee followed closely and saw the tomb and how his body was laid. They then went back and made ready spices and ointment. On the Sabbath they rested in accordance with the commandment, but on the first day of the week, Mary Magdalene, Joanna, Salome and Mary the mother of James bought spices, so that they might go and anoint Jesus.

They said to each other, "Who is going to roll away the stone for us from the entrance of the tomb?" But when they got there, they saw that the stone had been rolled back, only to find that the tomb was empty.

Standing in the tomb the three women looked puzzled, worried and began to cry frantically. "Oh no this cannot be, the tomb is empty," cried Joanna.

"That is impossible! What's happened, where is His body? He's gone; they have taken His body away," said Mary Magdalene. "But where - where could they have moved it? Wasn't it enough that they'd killed Him?" Joanna replied, "Don't cry, we'll find Him, I'm sure they couldn't have taken him very far. Maybe we've got the wrong tomb."

"No!" said Salome. "This is the right one; I'm sure it is. Look! Here is the linen he was wrapped in."
"Oh why?" Joanna said, "Why have they taken Him away? What did He do to deserve this? Why couldn't they just leave Him alone, He can't hurt anyone now that He's dead!" Mary said, "We just can't stand here – let's get some help. Let's go and tell the others."

The women left the tomb crying and sobbing as they went, totally oblivious to the fact that Mary Magdalene was still standing by the tomb. She looked into the tomb for the last time and surprisingly, saw a man dressed in white sitting there; unaware that he was an angel.
"Who are you? What are you doing here?" she asked.
"Woman," replied Saraqael, "Why are you crying?"
Mary Magdalene said with tears in her eyes, "Because

they have taken away the body of my Lord and I don't know where they have laid Him. Can you help me to find Him please? I must find Him!"

Saraqael said to Mary, "Why are you looking for the living among the dead? The one you're looking for is not here. He's alive!"

Still not understanding what the man was saying to her, or who he was, she went out of the tomb and there she saw another man.

"Sir," she said, who are you? Are you the gardener? What have you done with his body?" The man replied, "Woman! Why are you crying so? Who are you looking for?"

"Please, sir, if you have taken his body from here, tell me where it is so that I can take Him away," she said with her back towards the man crying.

Then she heard the voice she knew all too well, the voice she first heard back in the city of Magdala, a voice she could never forget, that delivered her from seven demons. "Mary," the voice said.

Joy filled her heart as she turned around shouting, "Jesus! Master! – It's you – it's really you." She moved forward to hug him, but in an instant, he stopped her.

"Do not touch me, because I have not yet ascended to the Father. But go and tell my disciples and Peter that I am ascending to my Father and your Father, to my God and your God."

Angels Awaiting News

Meanwhile, back in the heavenly realm, the angels are gathering together waiting in anticipation and excitement of the arrival of Archangel Gabriel, as he makes his way back from the planet earth. There is tension among them and they all want to know the news about their Lord. He entered the city with loud sounds of trumpets.

As soon as he entered, the angels swamped him with questions, after questions, after questions. One of the angels said,

"What mystery is going on? We have been waiting far too long. Tell us Gabriel. What's going on? It has now been thirty years, and nothing can replace our tears. Tell us Gabriel. What's going on?" Another said, "You're the master's right-hand man; surely you must know the plan? Tell us Gabriel, tell us Gabriel, we demand to know." Gabriel looked around him and said to the angels,

"Yes! Yes! Alas I must confess my friends the things that I now know. Our precious King, our sovereign Lord will soon come back home."

"When Gabriel? When is He coming home?"

"But not till He fulfils the words the prophets have foretold. Our King gave His life for men so that He may save their souls."

The angels repeated, "Save their souls?" Not really understanding. "Yes," Gabriel continued. "Remember back in the garden at the fall of man, they unknowingly handed the world to Lucifer and from that point, the fate of man was in his hands. But the Lord God's plan was far greater than we all could ever imagine. He said to the serpent back then, that the seed of a woman would retrieve it back.

"And remember how the prophets said that men would be redeemed with a perfect gift, a sacrifice, if only they would believe? That perfect gift is not the blood of goats or bulls or birds, the perfect gift that God could give was the blood of Emmanuel.... He has given His life as the perfect sacrifice. He has paid the price for man. Our Lord has conquered death and He has rose again." At this point the angels calmed down. Gabriel continues, "It was a mighty blaze of victory. Now all men shall know that forever He will reign. He shall appear to man. He shall be Lord of all."

One angel asked, "You mean He loves man so much, that He left his throne to die for them?"

"Yes," said Gabriel. "His love has no boundaries. His whole purpose from the very beginning was that man would be in fellowship with Him, once again.

Just as we are...